Praise for *How to Move*

The authors of this book bring together physiology, psychology and philosophy and make us look differently at the embedded routines of schooling and how schools could break out of teaching as they always have and improve learning for pupils in the future.

It is an energetic, highly readable and fascinating book which challenges thinking and practice in order to propose ways forward. Can schools step up, jump to it and take up the running ... or will they sit and watch the real world go by? This persuasive book will help those who want schools to be fit for purpose and our young people fit for learning.

Mick Waters, Professor of Education, University of Wolverhampton

As the pandemic created downward pressure on physical activity, this book could not have been timed more perfectly. In the quest for more physically active schools, classrooms and students, *How to Move & Learn* is the next must-have book on the topic! One of the great appeals of this project is how the authors align Move & Learn strategies with sound principles of instruction. The differentiation of Move & Learn Activators and Energisers is critical to classroom application. I was also impressed with the authors' examination of school and classroom culture and environment. We need to do more to recognise the absolute importance of movement in the teaching and learning process and this book takes us to the next level.

**Mike Kuczala, speaker, professional developer
and co-author of *The Kinesthetic Classroom* series**

This book is about changing learning and teaching for the better. The authors call for all educators to 'move and learn' with the times and ensure that physical activity is an everyday part of their lessons both outside and in – not simply something that happens during PE and playtimes.

The Move & Learn approach also values the benefits of play – both free play at playtimes as well as playful approaches to learning. It emphasises the need to consider the impact of the environment in which learning happens, including classroom, hall, corridors, playground, local green space and built environments.

Juliet Robertson, author of *Dirty Teaching* and *Messy Maths*

How to Move & Learn takes us into a journey of movement and its benefits. Through this text we are shown the importance and benefits of increased physical movement (and, in turn, decreasing sedentary times) on health, happiness and learning. Through this we see the potential flaw in generally expected classroom behaviour. We see that particularly in Western society most of our children are insufficiently active, and how through education we can change this. A strong case is made to show the impact of physical activity on learning – and it is a turnaround from what has traditionally been assumed; in fact, as the title suggests, movement and learning go hand in hand!

Now, the benefits of physical activity are not in themselves revolutionary – however, the knowledge that movement can increase the learning experience is. The book is a practical guide with strategies that can be not just put in place, but placed at the core of the learning environment.

Move & Learn is a joyous piece of work that gives us a sneaky peak into just how enriching a curriculum can be.

Chris Dyson, Head Teacher, Parklands Primary School

This book is timely and an essential read for all school-based Initial Teacher Education courses – indeed, a must for any teacher during their Early Career Framework period because they will find the ideas and examples help to extend their pedagogical repertoire of skills and knowledge. It should also be read by every primary head teacher before taking up post, since if they take note of the many examples and case studies in *How to Move & Learn* they will be even more successful – not just with improving children's learning but also the mental health and well-being of pupils and colleagues alike.

It's a super book and every teaching hub should be buying and distributing multiple copies.

Tim Brighouse, former Commissioner for London Schools

This is an interesting and timely book. It's a well-researched entry into the debate about how we should teach and learn and it is well worth a read. I love the balance it displays – something rare in the current climate. It is also a really good mix of the academic and the practical and a fine antidote to the 'sit down and learn' messages that we seem to be getting too often these days.

David Cameron, The Real David Cameron Ltd

While families are being told their children and young people need to be more active and healthy, the current educational trends decreed from on high are that they should sit still, follow the teacher with just their eyeballs and remain silent. In this delightful, timely and useful book, Bryn Llewellyn, Ian Holmes and Richard Allman offer us the research-informed, realistic and experience-led counterpoint to this sedentary state of affairs. *How to Move & Learn* is a powerful account of the benefits of enactive and active learning; a book that will be useful to anyone seeking the truth about and fun in learning. Get moving!

Hywel Roberts, travelling teacher, author and speaker

Finally we have a book which endorses what every teacher knows – children learn better when they move! Despite this, the majority of our lessons provide for sedentary learning. *How to Move & Learn* is not the usual must-read staffroom manual! It's like cosying under a heated blanket to watch a favourite movie on a cold, rainy Saturday afternoon. It's a comforting read, confirms what we know, helps us to understand why we teach as we do and what the research tells us about active learning – and, most importantly, it's packed with guidance on how we can change how we teach to integrate more movement into our lessons and trust ourselves to do what we know is right. I was one of hundreds of head teachers who worked with Bryn to integrate more movement into lessons throughout my school. We started with whole-staff training which, of course, included movement and we had 100% staff engagement with such incredible feedback that movement in every in-service training day became standard. Staff then found that in every lesson which planned for movement and learning there was 100% pupil engagement, improved behaviour for learning and increased attainment. It's not rocket science but getting started can feel overwhelming and *How to Move & Learn* is the perfect guide. I'd say it's a must-read for every staffroom library but as it's the perfect accompaniment for planning, preparation and assessment time, you will need several copies.

Alison Kriel, leadership consultant, keynote speaker and founder of Above & Beyond Education

How to

Move
& Learn

An Evidence-Based Guide to Embedding Physically Active Learning in Your School

Bryn Llewellyn, Ian Holmes and Richard Allman

Crown House Publishing Limited
www.crownhouse.co.uk

First published by
Crown House Publishing Limited
Crown Buildings, Bancyfelin, Carmarthen, Wales, SA33 5ND, UK
www.crownhouse.co.uk

and

Crown House Publishing Company LLC
PO Box 2223, Williston, VT 05495, USA
www.crownhousepublishing.com

© Bryn Llewellyn, Ian Holmes and Richard Allman, 2022

The right of Bryn Llewellyn, Ian Holmes and Richard Allman to be
identified as the authors of this work has been asserted by them in
accordance with the Copyright, Designs and Patents Act 1988.

First published 2022.

All photographs by Bryn Llewellyn with the following exceptions.
Page viii taken by Roger V. Moody, pages 45, 60 (top), 87 and 90 taken by Andy Morgan.

Cover images and images pages 4, 7, 10, 11, 14–15, 17, 19, 22–23, 29–31, 33–36, 58–59,
61, 75, 77, 93, 97–98, 112–113 and 115 © Buzz Burman.

Page 19: The Data Have Landed by Michael Rosen © 2017 from *Mr Mensh*
(Ripon: Smokestack Books). Used with kind permission.

Quotes from Ofsted and Department for Education documents used in this
publication have been approved under an Open Government Licence. Please see:
http://www.nationalarchives.gov.uk/doc/open-government-licence/version/3/.

British Library Cataloguing-in-Publication Data

A catalogue entry for this book is available from the British Library.

Print ISBN 978-178583631-2
Mobi ISBN 978-178583638-1
ePub ISBN 978-178583639-8
ePDF ISBN 978-178583640-4

LCCN 2022930829

Printed and bound in the UK by
CPi Antony Rowe, Chippenham, Wiltshire

Foreword

Why do we sit children down to learn?

As you let that question resonate, perhaps I might be able to shed light on the reason why. Since Victorian times, the school system has aligned to prepare children to succeed in exams. Sadly, the promotion of a testing culture has detrimentally impacted their physical, social and emotional health. Surely there has to be another way; an education system that values a child's holistic development, equally balancing their health with academic outcomes.

Despite COVID-19 shining a light on the wide-ranging importance of physical activity, the government narrative reinforced academic outcomes as the 'catch-up' priority,[1] largely ignoring students' physical and wider well-being needs and the ultimate impact they have on children's personal and academic development. Yet all is not lost; emerging from among the debris are pioneering teachers, schools and educational establishments who place their students' needs at the centre of the learning experience. While the term 'pioneer' is often bandied about, I do not use it lightly in reference to Bryn, Ian and Richard.

From our first encounter, Bryn showed passion and integrity in his mission to improve schools and classrooms. Having worked with over 300 schools, his knowledge and experience of embedding physically active learning (PAL) into everyday teaching practice is unrivalled. Six years on from our first meeting, I had the honour of presenting a TEDx Education talk on PAL with Bryn.[2] We called for a paradigm shift – this book could provide the impetus. Next, I met Ian, a pioneering head teacher who was prepared to rip up his school's timetable and integrate physical activity where most would least expect. Leading organisational change and building a new school culture that embraces physical activity takes time. Throughout his journey, Ian has shared his learning on an international stage and, more recently, has taken up the mantle of leading the implementation of the UK-based Creating Active Schools (CAS) Framework.[3] The final musketeer, Richard, was a pioneering

1   C. Scutt, 'Catch-up' and recovery approaches: selected reading, *Research Hub* (n.d.). Available at: https://my.chartered.college/research-hub/catch-up-and-recovery-approaches-selected-reading/.
2   B. Llewellyn and A. J. Daly-Smith, Physically active learning – improving performance [video], *TEDxNorwichED* (16 July 2018). Available at: https://www.youtube.com/watch?v=tARSCzHLF5g.
3   See https://www.creatingactiveschools.org.

teacher who empowered teachers within his school and wider trust to embrace physical activity approaches throughout the school day. As with Ian and Bryn, he sought to learn from evidence-based research and practice, to develop innovative solutions to support teachers – particularly in relation to the adaptation of classrooms and use of wider school spaces as active learning environments.

Leading a multi-country European project on school-based physical activity, I have met many PAL pioneers. The knowledge, skills and experience that Ian, Bryn and Richard possess place them at the forefront of international practice. To date, few teacher educators have bridged the research–practice gap. It is only by underpinning teaching practice with the latest research that we will make impactful and sustainable change within the education system. While their mission to embed PAL within schools has grown in prominence, it has not come without its challenges. In 2018, after the National Association of Head Teachers passed a motion to embrace PAL by 92%,[4] the national press was less convinced, writing 'Let children run around in class, headteachers told'.[5] What followed was a barrage of uneducated abuse – yet, undeterred, the musketeers stuck to their mission. The rich advice that follows in this book is testament to their perseverance and excellence.

How to Move & Learn seamlessly integrates research with rich practical experience from training teachers in over 400 schools. Beginning with teachers, the book draws on the latest behaviour change theory to support you to embrace PAL and integrate it within your teaching practice. What makes the Move & Learn concept unique is the integration of behaviour change theory and educational principles. Combined, they move PAL beyond its simplistic origins that aimed to get children moving more, to PAL's contribution as an engaging pedagogical approach within a more holistic educational experience. The beauty of this book resides in the bite-size chapters written to provide a teacher who is new to PAL with simple starter ideas. Similarly, the book will appeal to more advanced PAL practitioners who wish to enhance what they do and how they do it.

So, it is time to begin your Move & Learn journey. First, though, some tips I have learned through my work with teachers and schools on physical activity: start simple, have a go and don't give up if it doesn't work the first time. As you become

---

4 Tagtiv8, Trying to influence the decision makers – NAHT & beyond (n.d.). Available at: https://tagtiv8.com/influence-the-decision-makers/.
5 C. Turner, Let children run around in class, headteachers told, *The Telegraph* (May 2018). Available at: https://www.telegraph.co.uk/news/2018/05/04/let-children-run-around-class-headteachers-told/.

comfortable with PAL, read the final chapter; this focuses on taking a whole-school approach in order to create impactful and sustainable change in our schools. The vital lessons within this chapter will support you to look beyond your own teaching practice – hopefully empowering you to influence other key stakeholders (fellow teachers, senior leaders, parents) to adapt their approach to making physical activity an enjoyable and habitual part of every child's day.

All that is left to ask is a simple question: what will you do differently tomorrow to help your children Move & Learn?

Dr Andy Daly-Smith
Reader and co-director of the Centre for
Applied Educational Research, University of Bradford

Acknowledgements

As the saying goes, it takes a village to raise a child. The same can be said of creating and nurturing this book. Where do we start? At the beginning (a very good place to start); in this particular case it was Leeds – a city synonymous with leading the way, though not necessarily from the front.

As practitioners, we are well-versed in matters regarding school leadership and teaching. What we lacked were connections with researchers – local, national and international; step forward Dr Andy Daly-Smith, who kick-started the movement and has been an inspiration ever since. Further academic rigour and inspiration come courtesy of Dr Anna Chalkley, Dr Victoria Archbold and Professor Geir K. Resaland. Their robust research methods, explanations and support have certainly helped us understand more about behaviour change and how research can empower us to enhance practice for the benefit of more children.

We are indebted to school leaders and teachers for pioneering ideas and providing case studies:

- Paula Manser and her colleagues at Birkby Nursery and Infant School.
- Jez Whawell and his colleagues at Westerton Primary Academy.
- Alun Davies and teachers at Queensway Primary School and Melton Primary School.
- Chris Willan and his team at Water Primary School.
- Chris Dyson and all at Parklands Primary School.
- Chris Tolson, Niall O'Brien and the team at Academy St James' Bradford for championing PA and PAL locally and nationally.
- Nicola Roth and everyone at Lilycroft Primary School, Bradford.

Big shout-outs too to innovative individuals and organisations for your pioneering spirit and making time to talk with us:

- Jo Rhodes from Challenge 59.
- Henry Dorling.

- Juliet Robertson.

- HundrED.

- Michael Follett and the OPAL team.

We believe that you need to surround yourselves with awesome people who lift you up to a level beyond that which you thought you could achieve. With this in mind, we offer massive thanks to David Bowman and the team at Crown House Publishing – your patience knows no bounds. Thanks too to Buzz Burman for seeing things differently and creating the graphics.

Last, but by no means least, thank you to our families and friends for an ongoing blend of support and provocation:

- Kudos and hugs from Bryn to Dimitra, Joe, Ben, Andreas, Konstantinos, Robin and David.

- Ian is inspired every day by his amazing family and wants to thank his wonderful wife, Susie, and gorgeous children, Kathryn and Sam, for their unwavering support and patience. Without them this book would not have seen the light of day.

- Richard would like to thank the children, teachers, mentors and innovators that he's learned from since 2010.

Contents

Chapter 1

An Introduction to Move & Learn

To Move and/or Learn?

When we have asked those with whom we work, 'What does learning look like?', most responses for children over the age of 6 outline students sitting at desks focusing on a 'learning stimulus' (e.g. teacher with/without an interactive smartboard). However, if 'learning happens when people have to think hard',[1] as outlined by the Great Teaching Toolkit,[2] do we also have evidence showing that we can think harder when sedentary? We already know that increased physical activity and reduced sedentary time have wide-ranging benefits (including brain function), so what if we could show evidence that using movement in the learning process improves outcomes for children? What if we could then outline ways to support you (the practitioner) in adapting your practice to make this a reality? This book aims to do just that, providing you with the capability, opportunity and motivation to integrate movement purposefully into the learning process for those you teach. As teachers and school leaders, we have an opportunity to choose:

- An approach to learning that improves academic attainment as well as health and well-being outcomes, rather than seeing the two as mutually exclusive.

- To raise educational standards while bringing the joy of learning to our children.

- A culture of collaboration, curiosity and creativity.

- To be the teacher of the children who can't wait to tell others *how* and *what* they have learned today.

- To Move & Learn.

----

1 R. Coe, What makes great teaching?, *Centre for Evaluation & Monitoring* (31 October 2015), p. 13. Available at: https://www.ibo.org/globalassets/events/aem/conferences/2015/robert-coe.pdf.
2 See https://www.greatteaching.com.

Through this book – and our supporting continuing professional development (CPD) programme – we will:

- Highlight the benefits of Move & Learn and why you should incorporate it into your teaching and children's learning.

- Share knowledge, ideas and resources on how to integrate Move & Learn purposefully into lessons.

- Identify barriers to implementing Move & Learn and provide practical solutions.

- Connect practitioners to the latest research so that they can evolve their teaching practice in line with the most successful evidence-based approaches.

As a result, we seek to empower you and your school community to integrate movement as a key part of teaching and learning – to bring health and education together for the long-term benefit of the children we serve – to Move & Learn!

Move & Learn –
what it is and what it isn't

Strategies that integrate movement into learning have been around for a long time and are often referred to as PAL in both research and practice. PAL has recently been defined by researchers as 'the integration of physical activity into lessons in learning areas other than physical education (PE)'[3] and has been explored as a potential method of increasing activity in schools without detriment to educational time. If you walked into a staffroom or teacher training event and asked those present what PAL is and whether they had used such approaches with children in their class, you would probably get one or more of the following responses:

- 'Why would I want to let children run around the classroom? It would be dangerous and cause chaos!'

....

3 A. J. Daly-Smith, S. Zwolinsky, J. McKenna, P. D. Tomporowski, M. A. Defeyter and A. Manley, Systematic review of acute physically active learning and classroom movement breaks on children's physical activity, cognition, academic performance and classroom behaviour: understanding critical design features, *BMJ Open Sport & Exercise Medicine* 4(1) (2018): DOI.10.1136/bmjsem-2018-000341.

- 'Children get plenty of time to be physically active during break time, lunchtime, PE and clubs. They don't need it during lessons, especially not maths and English!'

- 'How am I meant to get them to sit down, listen and focus on their learning if they are being allowed to move?'

- 'Where can I fit this in? There's just not enough time in the day!'

- 'What about Ofsted? What will they say?'

These views are the first set of barriers to the successful implementation of Move & Learn strategies in any setting, and therefore it is essential to address both concerns and misconceptions so that they can be used purposefully and effectively by practitioners to enhance outcomes for children. Firstly, it is crucial that we understand what we mean by movement in the context of learning. Does it include:

- Sitting up straight – as we need to use our core muscles to do this?

- Handwriting – as we are moving our arms and hands, and again using our core muscles to sit appropriately?

- Other fundamental movement skills that we often see during PE lessons, school sport or through children's play (e.g. running, pushing, pulling, throwing, catching, balancing, climbing, digging)?

Let's consider this in the context of the widely accepted definition of physical activity: 'Any bodily movement produced by skeletal muscles that results in energy expenditure.'[4]

This already outlines that movement will sit on a spectrum, as a child will expend more energy playing tig for 15 minutes than they will sat still (although they may still be making minor movements to support the way they are sitting). However, this definition frames physical activity as a specific mechanistic act, and a recent paper has amended this definition for teachers, researchers and policy-makers to acknowledge the 'dynamic, complex and evolving array of reasons and emotions' involved in physical activity in the 21st century.[5] Piggin goes on to recommend

---

4   C. J. Caspersen, K. E. Powell and G. M. Christenson, Physical activity, exercise, and physical fitness: definitions and distinctions for health-related research, *Public Health Reports* 100(2) (1985): 126–131.
5   J. Piggin, What is physical activity? A holistic definition for teachers, researchers and policy makers, *Frontiers in Sports and Active Living* 2 (2020): 72.

that we consider physical activity as: 'People moving, acting and performing within culturally specific spaces and contexts, and influenced by a unique array of interests, emotions, ideas, instructions and relationships.'

We have used this definition in relation to our Move & Learn strategies, as it also explores the cognitive and emotive elements of physical activity, which are hugely relevant to its purposeful use in the learning process and for children in the 21st century. Its reference to spaces and contexts highlights the need for practitioners to consider the intensity and type of physical activity used when integrating movement into learning based on the relevant physical (e.g. classroom, hall, outdoor space) and social environments (e.g. class dynamics, staff dynamics) available. We can consider the spectrum of physical activity in a learning environment with some simple examples:

Sedentary – no or minimal physical activity	Light physical activity (LPA)	Moderate-to-vigorous physical activity (MVPA)
Sitting[6] – whether it be on the carpet, on a chair or at a desk	Balancing and stretching (body shapes) Casual walking/ movement over short distances for a short period of time	Brisk walking Running Skipping Climbing Digging Jumping Dancing Throwing and catching Pushing and pulling

6 Official definition also includes reclining and lying: M. S. Tremblay, S. Aubert, J. D. Barnes, T. J. Saunders, V. Carson, A. E. Latimer-Cheung et al., Sedentary Behavior Research Network (SBRN) – Terminology Consensus Project process and outcome, *International Journal of Behavioral Nutrition and Physical Activity* 14(1) (2017): 75.

We can then think about how appropriate the type of physical activity is to the physical environment (spaces and places available) and social environment (how children and teachers engage and support each other with the process) before deciding on how, when and whether it should be blended with academic content. You would never plan a running relay race in a classroom with desks, for example – whether they be in groups or rows – in order to collect facts on a new aspect of learning. You would need to take the learning to a more suitable space (hall or outdoors). Alternatively, if using the classroom, you might post facts on the walls and allow small groups of children to walk to collect them (modelling effective behaviour for others), before then sharing this information with the whole class. Taking into account these physical and social environmental factors, we would define the Move & Learn approach as a learning sequence that either directly or indirectly incorporates an appropriate type of physical activity to enhance the learner's development. We can unpick this definition further:

- **Learning sequence:** This highlights that we recognise it is unlikely that integrating movement for a whole lesson will genuinely benefit the learner; therefore, it is important to consider when in the process it is used and when being able to sit is actually more purposeful for learning.

- **Directly or indirectly:** This references the point that sometimes movement will be directly linked to the learning process (e.g. retrieving information from around a classroom to use in the next phase of learning), and sometimes movement will be indirectly linked (e.g. 5-minute movement break to allow children to reset and refocus during complex problem-solving tasks).

- **Appropriate type of physical activity:** This links to the type of movement (e.g. walking, running, jumping, stretching) and considerations of the physical and social environments in place.

- **Enhance the learner's development:** This is essential as, ultimately, by integrating movement, the learner should benefit more than they would by using traditional sedentary methods. This will hopefully be in relation to academic attainment, but provided academic attainment is not negatively impacted, the benefits could be related to improved focus, engagement, enjoyment and wider well-being.

We believe it is key that all of these elements are taken into consideration when planning how to Move & Learn, and we will explore this in more detail in Chapter 3. So, what does this look like in practice? This could be as simple as:

- A child making body shapes behind their desk to represent different multiple-choice answers when reviewing learning.
- A child doing star jumps on the spot in the classroom as they recite their four times tables.
- A child writing letters or words in chalk on a playground.
- A child building their own representation of a 2D or 3D shape using sticks, twigs and twine from the forest area.
- Children moving around the school grounds outside, searching for clues as a team to solve a problem.

Ultimately, Move & Learn is about finding opportunities to reduce sedentary time and increase physical activity while enhancing learning and the learning experience for children. The impact of this approach will be explored in more detail throughout this book, but for now just consider the following responses from teachers and children who have decided to embrace it.

During an outdoor maths session that involved children breaking place value numbers into separate movements, Mark Stephenson, a Year 3 teacher at Lanchester EP Primary School in Durham, revealed: 'I didn't know he could do that! He has never shown me that he understands that particular concept in a maths lesson or written it in his maths book.' According to Alun Davies, head teacher at Melton Primary School in Suffolk, this approach 'engages even the most reluctant of learners and inspires discussion beyond that achieved in the traditional classroom.' The reference to reluctant learners is an interesting one and seems to be borne out in the comments and feedback provided by children. According to Kian, a Year 5 child in Keighley: 'That game was awesome. It takes a lot to get me to do maths.'

Our Move & Learn approaches also seem to have an impact on changing attitudes to learning and confidence, particularly engaging reluctant learners in new ways of learning – as seen on the sweaty, happy face of Ethan, a Year 5 child in Leicester, at the end of an incredibly active session in the school hall: 'I used to think I was rubbish at maths, but now I know I'm not.' Why does this happen? As one higher level teaching assistant (HLTA) in Leeds said, 'I get this – it makes learning sticky.'

Our final quote, from Maisie, a Year 5 child in Bradford, brings us back to the Great Teacher Toolkit reference about learning, highlighted at the beginning of this chapter: 'I am so proud of myself. I didn't think I could think that hard.'

How to use this book to Move & Learn

Our intention is that this book is used to support your CPD in regard to implementing and embedding Move & Learn strategies into your practice. Different sections can be used depending on your needs or interests as a practitioner, and where you and your school are on your Move & Learn journey. We will achieve this by considering our Move & Learn culture and ethos, approaches, resources and environments (CARE) model:

Culture and ethos

We will examine the strategies and favourable conditions needed in an organisation's culture and ethos (including their vision and values) in order to recognise the benefits of Move & Learn and ensure that it is a key driver within a school's long-term improvement plan. This is covered in Chapter 2, where we will consider the perspective of a school's intent (vision), implementation and impact[7] in

7   Ofsted, *Education Inspection Framework* (May 2019), p. 9. Available at: https://www.gov.uk/government/publications/education-inspection-framework/education-inspection-framework.

relation to Move & Learn strategies, so that practitioners are confident that the quality of education they are providing is of the highest standard for those they teach.

Approaches, resources and environments

The ARE acronym in the education profession most commonly stands for 'age-related expectations' – a term that Ofsted, school leaders and teachers often focus upon. However, we think of ARE in terms of approaches, resources and environments; we will consider how Move & Learn strategies can be integrated into a high-quality teaching approach with supporting resources and adapted environments that still lead to the best possible outcomes for children. Chapters 3 and 4 explore the different ways Move & Learn strategies can be incorporated into existing teaching, and how they link with current pedagogy and evidence-based practice. Chapter 5 will highlight how to take these approaches into different environments, and also identify ways of adapting your school setting and setting up supporting resources in order to ensure effective delivery.

The CARE acronym was unintentional, but it certainly fits our Move & Learn agenda on many levels.

Whole systems change

Finally, in Chapter 6 we will reflect on how movement within curriculum lessons fits within the wider school context, considering the CAS Framework[8] and how to plan your own – and hopefully your school's – next steps to success in ensuring we all Move & Learn more often.

Moving along

At the end of every chapter, there is a section entitled 'Moving along'. This is your opportunity to explore the key points in the chapter with your colleagues and to think more deeply about how you can effectively implement this in your own setting. This may support senior leadership team (SLT) and/or other professional

----

8   A. J. Daly-Smith, T. Quarmby, V. S. J. Archbold, N. Corrigan, D. Wilson, G. K. Resaland et al., Using a multi-stakeholder experience-based design process to co-develop the Creating Active Schools Framework, *International Journal of Behavioral Nutrition and Physical Activity* 17 (2020): 13.

development meetings within your school and wider network. To help the process, we have used these headings:

- **Questions and tasks:** These are intended for SLT/CPD meetings.

- **Small steps, big difference:** Some simple suggestions to help you take the next step(s) on your Move & Learn journey. Consider this as your opportunity to implement a marginal-gains approach, as championed by Sir Dave Brailsford. This was used by the head of British Cycling to improve performance in tiny incremental steps, leading to success for the cyclists in the team.[9] Alun Davies, head teacher at Melton Primary School in Suffolk, says, 'it's easier to improve 20 things by 1% rather than one thing by 20%. It's more sustainable as it's less damaging to staff and less likely to have a negative impact on other areas. How often do we see schools have a big push on reading, writing or maths in sequence, only to see each one in turn drop off?'[10]

You may find it useful to document or record this process so that you can reflect and adapt your practice; this could be through a CPD log or by recording it on audio and/or video. Here is the first 'Moving along' section for you to work through:

---

9 J. Clear, This coach improved everything by 1 percent and here's what happened (n.d.). Available at: https://jamesclear.com/marginal-gains.
10 Personal correspondence.

Chapter 1	An Introduction to Move & Learn – Moving along

Questions & Tasks

1. Can you explain the definition of the Move & Learn approach to a colleague?

2. How do you personally feel about incorporating movement into your classroom/learning environment? Explore why with a colleague and draw up a list of both positives and potential challenges to overcome.

3. Can you think of ways you could incorporate movement purposefully into your teaching?

4. Watch the TEDx Talk entitled 'Physically Active Learning – Improving Performance'.[11] Talk about the content and issues with colleagues.

---

11 Llewellyn and Daly-Smith, Physically active learning – improving performance.

small steps
big difference

Based on what you have learned in this chapter, here are two simple ideas to try:

1. Take a small group of children and/or a colleague for a walk around the school grounds.

   › Discuss what they have learned so far that day and how they feel about it. This could be as part of a lesson or during break time.

   › Reflect on what you and they have got just from walking, talking and sharing.

2. Construct a simple line graph (see the following example) – the x-axis showing the time from the start to end of a school day, and the y-axis showing the level of physical activity (low to high). Draw a line to represent a typical day for your students. This line graph can be your baseline. Repeat this task as you implement different Move & Learn strategies to see the impact they have on the physical activity levels of the children. You could create a generic line graph for the school as a whole, or separate ones for each key stage/phase.

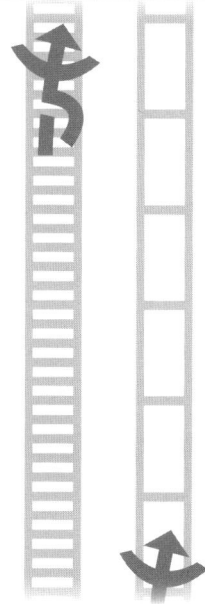

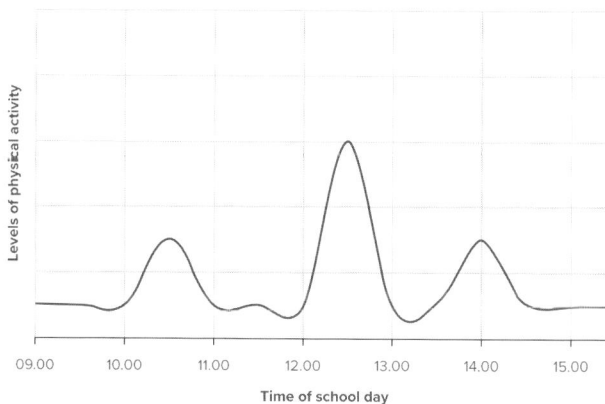

09.00   10.00   11.00   12.00   13.00   14.00   15.00

Time of school day

Levels of physical activity

Chapter 2

Culture and Ethos

A leap – why Move & Learn?
Why now? What is the intent?

The benefits of physical activity for all ages are wide ranging. It can improve physical health (cardio-respiratory, musculoskeletal and body mass) and mental health (positive self-esteem, lower levels of anxiety and stress). Physical activity also develops confidence, social skills and improves cognitive function and learning. However, the World Health Organization (WHO) has stated that one in four adults and three in four adolescents (aged 11–17 years) do not currently meet their global recommendations for physical activity.[1] Sport England's *Active Lives Children and Young People Survey*, published in December 2019, found that despite many interventions (including ongoing PE and sport premium funding), only 46.8% of children achieved the recommended daily levels of physical activity.[2] The UK guidance on physical activity for children and young people states that they should:

- Engage in moderate-to-vigorous intensity physical activity for an average of at least 60 minutes per day across the week.

- Engage in a variety of types and intensities of physical activity across the week to develop movement skills, muscular fitness and bone strength.

- Minimise the amount of time spent sedentary, and when physically possible should break up long periods of not moving with at least light physical activity.[3]

1   World Health Organization, *Global Action Plan on Physical Activity 2018–2030: More Active People for a Healthier World* (2018). Available at: https://apps.who.int/iris/bitstream/han dle/10665/272722/9789241514187-eng.pdf.
2   Sport England, *Active Lives Children and Young People Survey, Academic Year 2018/19* (December 2019). Available at: https://d1h1m5892gtkr7.cloudfront.net/s3fs-public/2020-01/active-lives-children-survey-academic-year-18-19.pdf?VersionId=cVMsdnpBoqROViY61iUjpQY6WcRyhtGs.
3   Department of Health & Social Care, Llwodraeth Cymru Welsh Government, Department of Health Northern Ireland and the Scottish Government, *UK Chief Medical Officers' Physical Activity Guidelines* (7 September 2019), p. 9. Available at: https://assets.publishing.service.gov.uk/government/uploads/system/uploads/attachment_data/file/832868/uk-chief-medical-officers-physical-activity-guidelines.pdf.

Source: https://www.thelancet.com/journals/lanchi/article/PIIS2352-4642(19)30323-2/fulltext

Given that the majority of children and young people do not accumulate the recommended 60 minutes of daily physical activity,[4] and with increasingly sedentary pursuits dominating leisure time,[5] the WHO and governments around the world have identified the essential role that schools can play in creating a more active society. For many years there has been physical activity guidance for children and young people to adhere to – however, less than 50% globally achieve this. Historically, the decline in physical activity behaviours was typically thought to occur in the teenage years. More recently, objective evidence suggests this gradual decline occurs much earlier. By the time most children begin their formal education, there is an average total physical activity decline of 4.2% per year (3.7% decrease in boys, 4.6% decrease in girls).[6] This has a further impact at age 7 (for those children who are classified as obese or overweight). This trend suggests that the displacement of MVPA and LPA to sedentary behaviours is now occurring at a younger age.

4 A. Cooper, A. Goodman, A. S. Page, L. B. Sherar, D. W. Eslinger, E. M. F. van Sluijs et al., Objectively measured physical activity and sedentary time in youth: the International Children's Accelerometry Database (ICAD), *International Journal of Behavioral Nutrition and Physical Activity* 12 (2015): 113.
5 S. Aubert, J. D. Barnes, C. Abdeta, P. A. Nader, A. F. Adeniyi, N. Aguilar-Farias et al., Global Matrix 3.0 physical activity report card grades for children and youth: results and analysis from 49 countries, *Journal of Physical Activity and Health* 15(2) (2018): 251–273.
6 Cooper et al., Objectively measured physical activity.

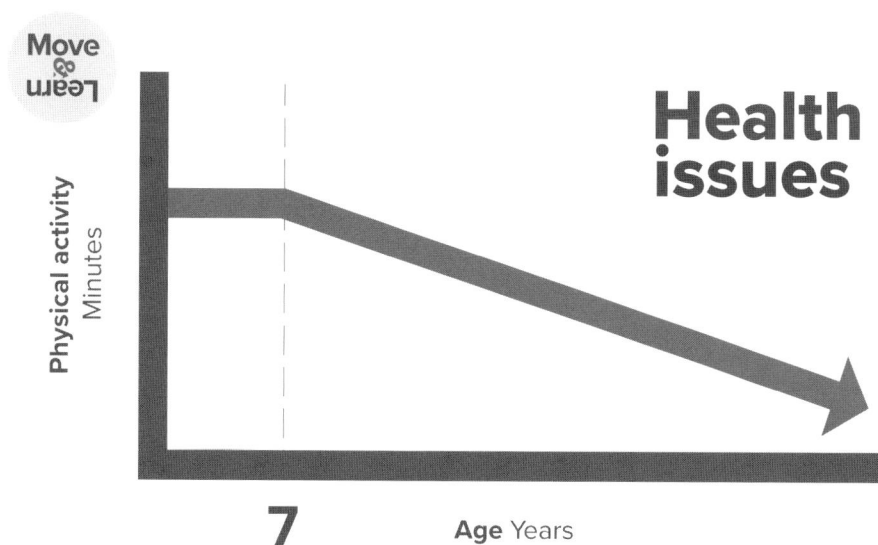

As to the reasons behind this decline, there is much speculation – from reduced opportunities to play and move freely as education is formalised (from Year 1 or 2 onwards in the UK) to increased access and reliance on digital devices. Unfortunately, a school day for children over 7 often consists of mostly seated lessons, with both boys and girls regularly only achieving a small percentage of MVPA at segmented points in the school day (e.g. break time, lunchtime, PE lessons).[7] In fact, a recent study showed that during a typical school day, less than 10% of children were achieving the recommended 30 minutes of MVPA per day in school.[8]

7   S. L. Taylor, W. B. Curry, Z. R. Knowles, R. J. Noonan, B. McGrane and S. J. Fairclough, Predictors of segmented school day physical activity and sedentary time in children from a northwest England low-income community, *International Journal of Environmental Research and Public Health* 14(5) (2017): 534.

8   A. J. Daly-Smith, M. Hobbs, J. L. Morris, M. A. Defeyter, G. K. Resaland and J. McKenna, Moderate-to-vigorous physical activity in primary school children: inactive lessons are dominated by maths and English, *International Journal of Environmental Research and Public Health* 18(3) (2021): 990.

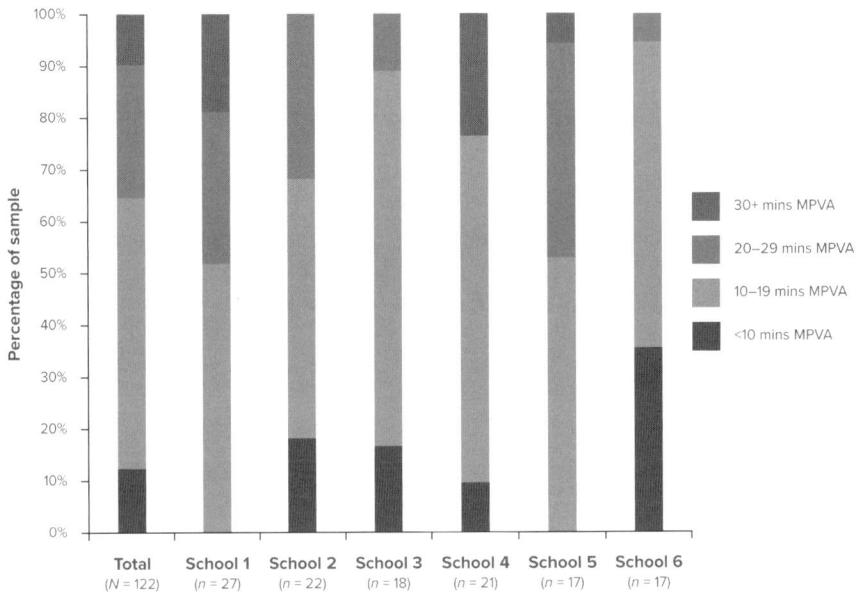

MVPA in primary school children: inactive lessons are dominated by maths and English.[9]

Add to this the fact that the UK's current strategy relies on children achieving 30 minutes of their daily physical activity at home too (which for many children, particularly disadvantaged, is often not the case) we are faced with a bleak picture that is impacting on children's well-being and attainment. This traditional 'seated' approach in education has created a tension in the development of our children and young people – attainment (e.g. Programme for International Student Assessment rankings[10]) vs well-being (e.g. WHO or national guidelines for physical activity). More often than not, teachers are asked to focus on ensuring children can read and write, are proficient in number and calculation and are provided with a curriculum rich in knowledge and experience; yet they are also continually asked to support the provision of the recommended amount of daily physical activity for children (*School Sport and Activity Action Plan*[11]) and be increasingly mindful of

9   Aubert et al., Global Matrix.
10   See https://www.oecd.org/pisa.
11   Department for Education, Department for Digital, Culture, Media & Sport and Department of Health & Social Care, *School Sport and Activity Action Plan* (July 2019). Available at: https://assets.publishing.service. gov.uk/government/uploads/system/uploads/attachment_data/file/848082/School_sport_and_activity_ action_plan.pdf.

their ever-growing mental health needs.[12] If only there was a way of learning that could address all of these issues ...

Research into how physical activity affects the brain has shown that it improves learning in the following ways: it 'optimises your mindset to improve alertness, attention and motivation ... prepares and encourages nerve cells to bind to one another, which is the cellular basis for logging in new information ... spurs the development of new nerve cells from stem cells in the hippocampus'.[13] There is also growing cross-sectional data to link physical activity and fitness with brain regions (e.g. the hippocampus) and networks integral to cognitive function and scholastic performance in children and adolescents.[14] Given this, and the fact that the hippocampus is the part of the brain involved in forming new memories and associated with emotions and learning, why do we not use it before or as an integral part of new learning challenges with children? If we refer back to the benefits of physical activity highlighted by the UK Chief Medical Officers, we can see there are many that link to improved learning for those we teach.[15]

Builds **confidence** and **social skills**

Maintains **healthy weight**

Makes **you feel good**

Improves **sleep**

Physical Activity

Benefits for children and young people (5–18 years)

Develops coordination

Improves health and fitness

Strengthens muscles and bones

Improves **concentration** and **learning**

12 Department for Education and Public Health England, *Promoting Children and Young People's Mental Health and Well-being: A Whole School or College Approach* (September 2021). Available at: https://assets. publishing.service.gov.uk/government/uploads/system/uploads/attachment_data/file/1020249/ Promoting_children_and_young_people_s_mental_health_and wellbeing.pdf.

13 J. J. Ratey and E. Hagerman, *Spark! How Exercise Will Improve the Performance of Your Brain* (London: Quercus Publishing, 2010), p. 55.

14 S. R. Valkenborghs, M. Noetel, C. H. Hillman, M. Nilsson, J. J. Smith, F. B. Ortega and D. Revalds Lubans, The impact of physical activity on brain structure and function in youth: a systematic review, *Pediatrics* 144(4) (2019): DOI.10.1542/peds.2018-403.

15 Sport England, *Active Lives Children and Young People Survey.*

Our message to children is often that physical activity helps to maintain a healthy weight (supported by a balanced diet) and improves health and fitness. However, if we linked more of the other benefits shown above to either readiness to learn (feeling good about yourself, improved sleep, strengthened muscles and bones so when they are sitting they can work and focus with good posture and therefore more effectively) or the learning process (develops coordination, improves concentration and learning), then we will quickly realise that incorporating physical activity across the school day will make for more prepared, engaged and effective learners. The beauty of Move & Learn is that it can be integrated over time into the curriculum, meaning that teachers are not having to find the time to fit something else in, which is often a challenge for the current profession. Research on the use of physical activity and PAL (the integration of physical activity into lessons in learning areas other than PE[16]) has shown the following:

● Children who have a higher level of physical fitness and are more physically active do better in maths, reading and overall academic scores.[17]

● PAL does not have a detrimental impact on academic performance, and in many cases has been shown to improve academic performance.[18]

● Longer-term studies where children have learned in active ways have shown four months of additional learning gains in maths and spelling compared to those who learn while sat down.[19]

● Studies have also established that PAL can benefit all demographic subgroups[20] and, in particular, boys and low-academic-performing girls.[21]

16 Daly-Smith et al., Systematic review.
17 J. W. de Greeff, R. J. Bosker, J. Oosterlaan, C. Visscher and E. Hartman, Effects of physical activity on executive functions, attention and academic performance in preadolescent children: a meta-analysis, *Journal of Science and Medicine in Sport* 21(5) (2018): 501–507.
18 E. Norris, T. van Steen, A. Direito and E. Stamatakis, Physically active lessons in schools and their impact on physical activity, educational, health and cognition outcomes: a systematic review and meta-analysis, *British Journal of Sports Medicine* 54 (2020): 826–838.
19 M. J. Mullender-Wijnsma, E. Hartman, J. W. de Greeff, S. Doolaard, R. J. Bosker and C. Visscher, Physically active math and language lessons improve academic achievement: a cluster randomized controlled trial, *Pediatrics* 137(3) (2016): 1–9.
20 J. B. Bartholomew, E. M. Jowers, G. Roberts, A. M. Fall, V. L. Errisuriz and S. Vaughn, Active learning increases children's physical activity across demographic subgroups, *Translational Journal of the American College of Sports Medicine* 3(1) (2018): 1–9.
21 G. K. Resaland, V. F. Moe, J. B. Bartholomew, L. B. Andersen, H. A. McKay, S. A. Anderssen and E. Aadland, Gender-specific effects of physical activity on children's academic performance: the Active Smarter Kids cluster randomized controlled trial, *Preventive Medicine* 106 (2018): 171–176.

● Immediately after being physically active, children have a greater focus on the task in hand.[22]

Therefore, the 'leap' referred to in the title of this chapter is not head teachers and teachers asking why, but why not? Sadly, for many school leaders and governors, pressures from government ministers and regulatory bodies mean that many schools globally deliver a narrow curriculum. With a government driven by data, many children are forced to subsist largely on a diet of English and mathematics. Studying for and to the test may work for certain children. However, many simply become lost in the system of accountability. This is captured by Michael Rosen in his poem, 'The Data Have Landed':

First they said they needed data about the children to find out what they're learning.

Then they said they needed data about the children to make sure they are learning.

Then the children only learned what could be turned into data.

Then the children became data.

Why do our children need to sit down to be good listeners and learners? Children may be sitting down, calm and looking at the teacher, but are they actually learning anything or achieving anywhere near their full potential for the duration of a lesson? It's not surprising that recent studies have explored how schools can

22 Daly-Smith et al., Systematic review.

effectively use standing desks to reduce sedentary time in our essentially Victorian-style classrooms.[23] While this solution may involve quite a radical change to the current environment (and has cost implications too) there are many other low-cost/no-cost solutions that can kick-start schools on their Move & Learn journey. So, what if Move & Learn was a way of not only improving standards, but also enriching the curriculum and bringing the joy of learning back to both children and teachers alike?

We have already outlined the positive effects of Move & Learn through the research, but we need to consider how we translate and model this for leaders and practitioners, so they see for themselves that by implementing movement into learning, the goals of attainment and well-being are not mutually exclusive. Programmes across the globe (e.g. Action Schools BC!,[24] Finland's Schools on the Move,[25] Norway's Active Smarter Kids[26] and the Center for Fysisk Aktiv Learning's (SEFAL)[27] Teacher Education programme and, more recently, the UK's CAS Framework (see Chapter 6)) are already integrating movement into learning as part of a whole-school approach to increasing physical activity across the school day. The UK government has also recommended 'building in activity to classroom lessons … [to boost children's] physical health, mental well-being, character and resilience' in its *School Sport and Activity Action Plan*.[28] The CAS Framework recognises active curriculum lessons as the most effective strategy in increasing physical activity across the school day, because in addition to the benefits already highlighted earlier, active lessons:

- reach *all* students.

- are directly controlled by the teacher.

- impact on the most sedentary part of the school day.[29]

23 S. A. Clemes, S. E. Barber, D. D. Bingham, N. D. Ridgers, E. Fletcher, N. Pearson et al., Reducing children's classroom sitting time using sit-to-stand desks: findings from pilot studies in UK and Australian primary schools, *Journal of Public Health (Oxford, England)* 38(3) (2016): 526–533; E. Hinckson, J. Salmon, M. Benden, S. A. Clemes, B. Sudholz, S. Barber et al., Standing classrooms: research and lessons learned from around the world, *Sports Medicine* 46(2) (2016): 297; Y.-L. Chen, K. Tolfrey, N. Pearson, D. D. Bingham, C. Edwardson, L. Cale et al., Stand out in class: investigating the potential impact of a sit–stand desk intervention on children's sitting and physical activity during class time and after school, *International Journal of Environmental Research and Public Health* 18(9) (2021): 4759.
24 See https://actionschoolsbc.ca/.
25 See https://schoolsonthemove.fi/.
26 See https://www.activesmarterkids.com/.
27 See https://www.hvl.no/en/about/sefal.
28 Department for Education et al., *School Sport and Activity Action Plan*.
29 Daly-Smith et al., Using a multi-stakeholder experience-based design process.

The promising news is that internationally there is recognition that the system has to change, and this has recently been drawn together in an umbrella review with the WHO, which includes the recommendation that teachers should be trained in how to enhance physical activity across the school day, including active classrooms.[30]

However, despite the research, policy and frameworks available, the uptake within schools is still relatively slow – this is particularly the case in the UK due to an education system full of competing priorities. There continues to be a tension between movement and learning when, actually, the research and science show that the two go hand in hand. Many adults, whether they be teachers, parents or government ministers, still consider this approach as less formal learning, with less achieved in the lessons. However, perceptions are changing – the research is showing that when implemented successfully, it's a case of quality (engaging purposeful learning) over quantity (time spent sitting at a desk writing or listening, but not necessarily learning). Therefore, to ensure effective implementation and sustainable change for children, practitioners will require carefully managed and strategically planned small steps.

Small steps – how to implement Move & Learn effectively

We can share all the amazing research in the world but Move & Learn will not be implemented if it is not seen as a purposeful priority by schools, teachers and wider policy-makers. Therefore, before considering how to model it effectively in practice, it is essential to consider the perceived barriers and challenges of integrating movement into lessons, which schools and teachers have raised. When researchers have reviewed studies into teachers' perceptions, the main barriers to implementation include:

- Lack of knowledge and training in relation to the benefits of PAL and how to implement PAL successfully.

- Impact on behaviour and ability to manage their class.

---

30 A. Barbosa, S. Whiting, P. Simmonds, R. Scotini Moreno, R. Mendes and J. Breda, Physical activity and academic achievement: an umbrella review, *International Journal of Environmental Research and Public Health* 17(16) (2020): 5972.

- Lack of time to prepare and implement the programme.

- A shortage of appropriate space or resources for delivery.

- Resistance from parents, other teachers and senior leaders.[31]

These are all challenges that can be overcome with investment in high-quality and continued professional development on:

- Approaches (Chapter 3 and Chapter 4).

- Environments and resources (Chapter 5).

- The involvement of all stakeholders (including parents) on the journey (Chapter 6).

This can be achieved using the capability, opportunity, motivation and behaviour (COM-B) model:[32]

This model is now used extensively in behaviour change interventions and recognises that behaviour is part of an interacting system involving the components of capability, opportunity and motivation. Interventions need to change one or more

31 A. J. Daly-Smith, T. Quarmby, V. S. J. Archbold, A. C. Routen, J. L. Morris, C. Gammon et al., Implementing physically active learning: future directions for research, policy and practice, *Journal of Sport and Health Science* 9(1) (2020): 41–49; A. J. Daly-Smith, J. L. Morris, E. Norris, T. L. Williams, V. Archbold, J. Kallio et al., Behaviours that prompt primary school teachers to adopt and implement physically active learning: a meta synthesis of qualitative evidence, *International Journal of Behavioral Nutrition and Physical Activity* 18 (2021): 151.
32 S. Michie, M. V. S. Maartje and R. West, The behaviour change wheel: a new method for characterising and designing behaviour change interventions, *Implementation Science* 6 (2011): 42.

of them in such a way as to put the system into a new configuration and minimise the risk of it reverting.

The behaviour change wheel[33]

Let's take each area in turn.

Capability

The capability to change is influenced by two factors:

1   **Physical:** Do teachers know how to change? How hard/easy do they find change?

2   **Psychological:** Do teachers think they might decide to change or not to do so? Why? Do they think they will be able to do so? (Perceived competence)

In terms of teachers' capability to implement Move & Learn approaches, examples of how this could be increased include:

● Modelling effective Move & Learn lessons as part of a teacher training course.

● Peer coaching and mentoring used to support teachers in delivering effective Move & Learn lessons, adapting their lessons together to improve movement and attainment.

---

33 Michie et al., The behaviour change wheel.

Opportunity

Opportunity is influenced by two environments:

1 **Physical environment:** Do teachers have the resources they need to deliver Move & Learn approaches? How will they make time to deliver Move & Learn approaches?

2 **Social environment:** What do teachers' peers think about prioritising Move & Learn approaches? Do they know who has done this successfully?

In terms of teachers' opportunity to implement, examples of how this could be increased include:

● Timetabling hall time for specific year groups to improve space available for Move & Learn approaches.

● Incorporating the use of movement within lesson times as part of school policy (e.g. teaching and learning, class rules and routines).

Motivation

Teacher motivation is influenced by:

1 **Identity:** How compatible are Move & Learn approaches with their professional values and responsibilities?

2 **Beliefs:** How confident are they? What do they think will happen if they do it/don't do it?

3 **Emotion:** When they think about Move & Learn approaches, what feelings come up?

4 **Goals:** How much do they want to incorporate Move & Learn approaches? Do Move & Learn approaches align or conflict with other things they want to do?

In terms of teachers' motivation to implement, examples of how this could be increased include:

● Understanding different teachers' barriers (e.g. negative emotional responses to physical activity, belief that they will lose control of behaviour in their class) and then addressing these through structured support (e.g. providing relevant training (capability) and opportunity (peer support)).

- Setting goals for teaching staff (e.g. working towards an effective increase in their use of movement in lessons) and incorporating them into CPD meetings (informal) or performance-management objectives (formal).

Whatever you do and at whatever level (e.g. SLT, subject, year group), do so in small steps. Make sure each step is purposeful (supports high-quality teaching) and is successful (leads to improvements in learning outcomes and increases movement) before implementing the next phase of the strategy. From our experience, the first small step for practitioners is to establish clear routines and structures (as with any good teaching and learning approach). This way, everyone involved knows what, when and how movement is being used in lessons. Some schools have supported this need for structure/routine by simply adapting the length of lessons and incorporating physically active breaks as a way of shifting the culture in school to a day that involves more moving and less sitting. Once children are used to these new routines, it has then proved easier to begin to adapt lessons, or parts of lessons, to incorporate movement too. Equally, if capacity to deliver training with all staff or competing priorities within a school reduce the time available to support Move & Learn approaches, it can also be useful to start implementation with the early years foundation stage (EYFS), where movement through the day is already a natural part of the curriculum, and then work up through the school. In effect, this means that as children progress through the year groups, they are already used to a culture of moving and learning. We have included an overview audit tool to start you on your Move & Learn journey in Appendix 1 (see page 115). This includes examples of small steps that can be taken to increase your capability, opportunity and motivation to use movement in your lessons to inspire a generation of movers and learners!

As with any new initiative, teachers need time to use training to gradually and continually adapt their practice to ensure it is having a positive, sustainable impact on outcomes for the children. Therefore, we would argue that the best possible resource investment a school can make in implementing Move & Learn approaches is to give teachers the time to collaborate with others, and observe and develop best practice. By doing this, teachers will be able to adapt their own plans and pedagogy in small steps so that Move & Learn approaches become an integral part of the way they teach and their children learn. This could take the form of setting up peer mentors so that staff can work together to adapt their planning and delivery in small steps, ensuring that Move & Learn approaches are regularly on staff meeting agendas (you could even deliver staff meetings using Move & Learn strategies!), or additional time out of class to observe best practice – either in your own or another school's setting. As time is at a premium, teachers often look for quick fixes in the form of ready-made resources and new equipment. But it is investment in schools' most important resource (staff) that will ensure Move & Learn approaches genuinely transform both teaching and learning in your school.

A sense of balance – how to monitor the impact of Move & Learn

Let's start with a health warning. We've referenced the importance of small steps in relation to implementation, and it is key to remember this when evaluating the impact of Move & Learn on children, staff and your school. Successfully incorporating Move & Learn approaches does not mean that every lesson of every day should involve movement. Think of the NHS Couch to 5K running plan[34] – small steps will lead to small levels of impact and, provided this is noticeable and moving in the right direction (through improved engagement, focus and – dare we say – student enjoyment), this is progress. We need to always bear in mind the long-term trajectory.

Teachers will need time to set new routines and expectations and take risks, adapting their practice alongside colleagues and ongoing training to ensure it works for both the children's well-being and attainment. Leaders will need to provide regular support, challenge and recognition (in equal measure) and see Move & Learn approaches as a genuine school-improvement priority. In monitoring and evaluating, it may be useful to use sets of activity trackers and standardised assessments as quantitative measures of progress, while not forgetting that children should not be obsessed with data but with the joy of moving and learning. If you do decide to use activity trackers, we would recommend using them sparingly – for example, don't feel the need to invest in them for every class, but use with one year group for a few weeks before rotating on to a different one, eventually revisiting the year groups again at some point during the academic year. This ensures children don't become either obsessed/demotivated/oblivious to the trackers and that you are not constantly 'weighing the pig', giving time for change to embed and physical

---

34 NHS, Couch to 5K: week by week (n.d.). Available at: https://www.nhs.uk/live-well/exercise/couch-to-5k-week-by-week/.

activity levels to improve. For qualitative measures, observations of learning and play, feedback from children, staff and parents (through discussions or surveys) will all contribute to a judgement and reflection of how Move & Learn has been embedded since the initial audit. Again, think here about how to integrate these into the curriculum (rather than as an additional monitoring task for staff) – for example, at the beginning and end of each half term children could discuss movement across the school day as part of their reflections in a PE lesson, given that two of the overarching aims for students are:

- To ensure they are physically active for sustained periods of time.

- To lead healthy, active lives.

The audit tool in Appendix 1 (see page 115) provides practical advice for ongoing monitoring. As with any initiative, the effective monitoring and evaluation of how Move & Learn is being delivered is crucial to its purposeful and successful implementation. And while we talk of balance, it is fundamental to remember we are not advocating that by being physically active, everything has to be at a fast and furious pace.

Should everything be done in an active way? The answer is no. But actually being able to put one or two active learning lessons into a week to start off with – and it doesn't need to be a whole lesson, it could be small parts of lessons – for those children who are scared by literacy or numeracy, to do it in an active way can sometimes take away those barriers that they face in a traditional setting.[35]

---

35 A. J. Daly-Smith, LBU research into physically active learning (ITV Calendar News) [video], *Tagtiv8* (20 July 2018). Available at: https://youtu.be/Rd3hcPbYbss.

Children will still need independent time at their desks (sitting or standing) and sedentary time to reflect. In addition, we need to acknowledge that some children may have their own fears and inhibitions in relation to physical activity itself; therefore, it's important to gradually introduce supportive and non-threatening movement-based learning so that all children benefit from this approach. This links back to the COM-B model (see page 22) and capability, opportunity and motivation in relation to children's physical activity:

Capability

- If a child is more capable of performing physical activity, they are more likely to continue to participate in it.
- Increased capability increases their motivation to complete physical activity by choice.

Opportunity

- Greater opportunity for physical activity means greater likelihood of participating in physical activity and greater motivation.
- Increasing opportunity means that more physical activity is practised, boosting capability.

Motivation

- Motivation is based on wants/needs and evaluations of situations. To get children active, it must be suited to their wants/needs/interests at the time.
- Children act on the values they have witnessed or lived by – praise and acceptance of activity can motivate a child to participate or continue with the related activity.

In fact, the balance of movement and being still is vital in the 21st-century world our children will be sharing and shaping. Let's teach them to be active participants in learning and life, while recognising the need to regularly slow down, take a step back and reflect. Let's help them to reflect on their achievements and how to find the right pathway in a world where it seems that decisions (and learning outcomes) need to be made instantaneously.

We often talk in education about ensuring children access a broad and balanced education. What if physical activity and wider well-being were essential parts of that breadth and balance?

Well-being					
Physical activity					
Nature and outdoors	**Mental health**	**Nutrition**	**Sleep**	**Relationships**	**Identity** (Including interests, hobbies and beliefs)
Broad and balanced curriculum (incorporating movement)					
Happy, healthy, achieving child					

A new perspective on a broad and balanced curriculum

What if physical activity was the driver used to support many other well-being aspects, educating on how physical activity:

- Enhances our ability to experience nature and the great outdoors?
- Can be used to manage our mental well-being?
- Can be used alongside interventions to ensure healthy nutrition and healthy weight?
- Improves sleep (vital for well-being and learning)?
- Improves relationships through social connections and bringing communities together?
- Can give us a sense of identity through finding our passion for movement (whether this be gardening, walking or more organised sport)?

What if all teachers incorporated movement into the broad and balanced curriculum – not only promoting the benefits of physical activity, but ensuring the right balance between movement and sedentary time across the school week? What if all children were happier, healthier and higher achieving?

Moving along

Chapter 2	Culture and Ethos – Moving along

Questions & Tasks

1. Why do you create so many opportunities for children to sit down during the school day? What parts of the lesson do children actually need to be sitting down for?

2. How do you know a child is learning when they are sitting still and listening? Consider students' perceptions of learning and how Move & Learn approaches might increase engagement and attention.

   > Ask children to explain or draw what learning in the classroom looks, sounds and feels like for them. This could be done for individual classes but also across the whole school.

   > Explain to children they learn best when they have to think hard – do they agree, and if so, when does this happen for them?

   > List the benefits from increasing the amount of movement in the classroom (referring back to the scientific and research evidence provided in this chapter if required).

   > Consider the evidence you have collected; which do you find the most persuasive as a trigger for evolving your own practice?

3. What expectations do you set for physical activity or sedentary behaviour in your classroom?

4. Discuss your own perceptions of barriers/challenges on implementing Move & Learn approaches and then identify practical solutions with a colleague (linking back to your answers for Q1 to Q3).

5. With staff, complete the Move & Learn audit tool (Appendix 1 on page 115) to baseline where your school is on the journey. Prioritise simple ideas (small steps, big difference) and ensure these are referenced in your whole-school improvement plan. Revisit this each half term with staff and prioritise the sharing of best practice and lessons learned using the COM-B model.

small steps
big difference

Based on what you have learned in this chapter, here are three simple ideas to try:

1. Before starting the next chapter, identify one small step you could take to reduce sedentary time each day for your class, while retaining (and even increasing) engagement for children in your lessons.

2. Use the line graph you drew in Chapter 1 to support your reflections on this.

3. Based on our 'broad and balanced' curriculum diagram on page 29, review your weekly timetable, and consider whether you have the right balance between sedentary time and movement. Plan in one or two activities to try with your class to reduce sedentary time and reflect on the impact of these over several weeks.

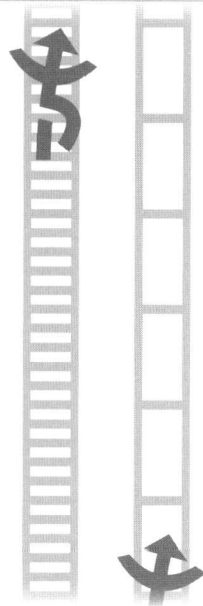

Chapter 3

Move & Learn Approaches

If implemented successfully, movement should, over time, simply become part of a high-quality teaching and learning process. In this chapter, we will explore our Move & Learn approaches that will support teachers in integrating movement into their teaching and children's learning, which have been developed from our definition:

A Move & Learn approach is a learning sequence that either directly or indirectly incorporates an appropriate type of physical activity to enhance the learner's development.

We will therefore need to consider the different direct and indirect strategies that a teacher can use (the how), and the part of the teaching and learning sequence to use them (the when) to ensure that movement purposefully and effectively improves outcomes for the children being taught.

How and when can Move & Learn be used to support and enhance learning?

In considering the most appropriate approaches to use to support both movement and learning within a lesson, it is key that practitioners understand whether the movement will be directly or indirectly incorporated into the teaching and learning process.

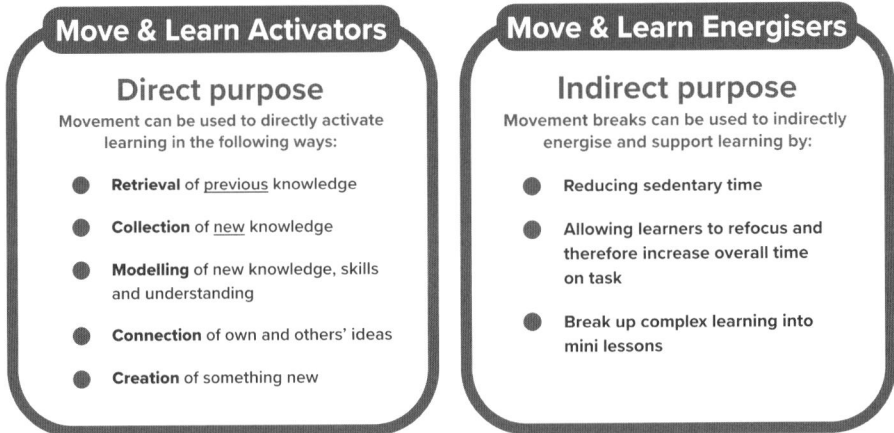

Move & Learn Activators	Move & Learn Energisers
Direct purpose	**Indirect purpose**
Movement can be used to directly activate learning in the following ways:	Movement breaks can be used to indirectly energise and support learning by:
● **Retrieval** of <u>previous</u> knowledge	● Reducing sedentary time
● **Collection** of <u>new</u> knowledge	● Allowing learners to refocus and therefore increase overall time on task
● **Modelling** of new knowledge, skills and understanding	
● **Connection** of own and others' ideas	● Break up complex learning into mini lessons
● **Creation** of something new	

Direct purpose (Move & Learn Activators)

These are approaches that integrate movement directly into a learning sequence, making children (both literally and psychologically) active participants in their learning. Our five direct-purpose approaches are:

● **Move & Learn Retrieval:** Retrieving existing knowledge or concepts learned.

● **Move & Learn Collection:** Collecting new knowledge or stimuli to support learning.

● **Move & Learn Modelling:** Using movement to model or represent concepts.

● **Move & Learn Connection:** Moving to connect ideas and thoughts in order to put knowledge and concepts into context.

● **Move & Learn Creation:** Moving to create and demonstrate knowledge, skills and understanding.

Before we explain each approach in detail, it's important to outline when these might be used in the learning process. In our own teaching practice, we have used the structure of observed learning outcomes (SOLO) taxonomy;[1] a model that describes levels of increasing complexity in students' understanding of subjects as a useful tool in the design of lessons.[2] The various stages of this taxonomy can be described as on page 36.[3]

As we want to ensure that movement is an integrated and purposeful part of the learning process, we have linked our Move & Learn approaches to the relevant stages of SOLO in the following table, so that teachers can see:

● How they relate to helping move children on in their learning.

● At which point in a learning sequence to use each approach.

Move & Learn	Prestructural	Unistructural	Multistructural	Relational	Extended abstract
Retrieval	☑	☑	☑		
Collection	☑	☑	☑		
Modelling	☑	☑	☑		
Connection				☑	
Creation					☑

1 J. B. Biggs and K. F. Collis, *Evaluating the Quality of Learning: The SOLO Taxonomy (Structure of the Observed Learning Outcome)* (New York: Academic Press, 1982).
2 Almondbury High School and Language, Focus: Hattie's effect sizes; SOLO taxonomy, *The Pupil*, 2nd edn (September 2013). Available at: http://www.asdn.org/wp-content/uploads/hattie-and-solo-The-Pupil.pdf.
3 Adapted from National College for Teaching & Leadership, *Beyond Levels: Alternative Assessment Approaches Developed by Teaching Schools – Research Report* (2014), p. 13. Available at: https://assets. publishing.service.gov.uk/government/uploads/system/uploads/attachment_data/file/349266/ beyond-levels-alternative-assessment-approaches-developed-by-teaching-schools.pdf. Originally adapted from P. Hook and J. Mills, *SOLO Taxonomy: A Guide for Schools Book 1* (New Zealand: Essential Resources Educational Publishers, 2011).

Prestructural	Unistructural	Multistructural	Relational	Extended abstract
	Remembering/ knowing & understanding	Remembering/ knowing & understanding	Applying & analysing	Evaluating & creating
Children don't really have any understanding or knowledge of the topic being studied.	Information makes sense but children have limited knowledge.	Children have a range of information but meta connections between the information and learning are not made.	Children see the significance of how various learning and knowledge relate to one another. Children are able to link together and explain several ideas around a related topic.	Children can make connections beyond the scope of the problem or question. They generalise or transfer learning into a new situation. They can also link learning to other bigger ideas and concepts.

Additional explanation on how these approaches link to SOLO taxonomy is provided further on.

Indirect purpose (Move & Learn Energisers)

These are approaches that are used to provide children with a chance to refocus or to support their transition between lessons or parts of lessons. These still need to be carefully prepared, with clear routines and expectations in place to ensure they achieve their purpose of re-engaging children effectively for the next part of their learning, as well as making them more physically active. These are often known as active breaks, but we prefer Move & Learn Energisers – moving to refocus and recharge, ready for the next phase of learning. We will now go through each Move & Learn approach in more detail, giving examples of how they can be practically implemented into part of a lesson.

Please note – our approach (and this book) is not about providing practitioners with off-the-shelf lesson plans or a scheme of work to follow. Our belief is that while this may take practitioners and schools longer to implement, it will be more sustainable as it becomes part of their core pedagogy and can be adapted to each school's context and curriculum.

Move & Learn Activators and Energisers

Move & Learn Retrieval

A key to ongoing learning is to ensure that children regularly revisit prior content so that:

1   Their learning is scaffolded and they can build on what they know (Vygotsky's Zone of Proximal Development[4]).

2   Information can be automatically recalled from long-term memory with minimal conscious effort. This automation reduces the burden on working memory (which is limited), freeing it up to learn new information.[5]

Therefore, retrieval of prior knowledge at the start of a learning sequence is key to successful outcomes. As retrieval is the process of getting something back from somewhere, movement can be integrated with ease into this part of a lesson in the following ways:

- Physically retrieving information or objects from somewhere in the learning environment – for example:

  › A range of vocabulary linked to any subject could be spread around a learning environment and a number of children (size of group would depend on the space available) could then collect a word they know the meaning of. Children could then explain the meaning to the rest of the class and even post it on a memory-quadrant display (e.g. *what I learned yesterday, last week, last term, last year*). Words that are not collected may then need to be explained by the teacher or their peers, so that all children are aware of the key concepts before starting the new material.

  › Answers to set questions of content previously covered by the class could be scattered around the learning environment and children would have to match the correct answer to the question.

---

4   L. S. Vygotsky, *Mind in Society: The Development of Higher Psychological Processes* (Cambridge, MA: Harvard University Press, 1978).

5   NSW Government, *Cognitive Load Theory: Research that Teachers Really Need to Understand* (5 September 2017). Available at: https://www.cese.nsw.gov.au/publications-filter/cognitive-load-theory-research-that-teachers-really-need-to-understand.

> Relevant artefacts from a wider range of available items for history or religious education, or relevant equipment/materials for geography, science, art or design and technology could be retrieved from different places at the beginning and/or end of the learning sequence to demonstrate knowledge gained.

- Using movement to recall basic number or word facts, for example:
  > Children could recite different times tables with a partner on the spot using simple movement (e.g. recall the five times table while standing up and using high fives with their partner).

  > Children could move around the space and use rhythm as they move (e.g. each step is a letter or phoneme) to spell out the parts of taught spellings.

  > Children could move around the space and use different movements to recall key number facts (e.g. hop for odd numbers, jump for even numbers or hop over words spelt incorrectly and jump over words spelt correctly). This activity would probably need to be done in a hall space or outdoor space, so could be used immediately before or after play.

- Moving to a part of the room or moving a part of their body as answers to questions. Retrieval through questioning and low-stake quizzes has proved to enhance learning,[6] and this is a fun and engaging way for teachers to quickly determine children's prior knowledge (including any gaps or misconceptions), for example:
  > A teacher gives four possible answers to a question, represented by the four corners of the learning environment. Children then move to the part of the room they think represents the correct answer.

  > The class agrees to four different yoga poses to represent the A, B, C and D optional answers to questions. The teacher then asks or displays each question and the children have to pick the relevant yoga 'response'.

In both these scenarios, this is also a useful tool for a teacher to identify (in a sensitive way) children that may have gaps or misconceptions, as they can observe which children have delayed responses or copy others, and then follow up through either targeted questioning or one-to-one support as appropriate. Effective

---

6   J. D. Karpicke and P. J. Grimaldi, Retrieval-based learning: a perspective for enhancing meaningful learning, *Educational Psychology Review* 24 (2012): 401–418.

teacher questioning after this activity is still a fundamental part of the teaching and learning process, as it supports the teacher in identifying children that need further support. This approach is clearly linked to the unistructural and multistructural aspects of SOLO taxonomy, in that it will highlight if children can remember one or multiple aspects of prior learning, but will not necessarily show if they have made connections between them. It will also support the prestructural aspect, as it will identify those that have not confidently retained any prior knowledge on a given subject in their long-term memory.

Move & Learn Collection

This is about children collecting ideas to support their understanding of new knowledge and skills. This is similar to the retrieval activities, but rather than children moving to retrieve information they have already been taught, this is about children moving to collect new information and ideas. Again, if we consider that collection is about fetching, systematically acquiring and gathering together, then we can explore practical ways it can be used, as follows:

- Children move in different ways (depending on the available space and number of children) to collect key concepts that will, with carefully planned teacher support, enable them to investigate and explore their understanding and go on to make deeper connections with the learning content, for example:
  - When gathering ideas for independent writing, children move around the classroom collecting specific word classes/phrases spread around the learning environment.
  - Children collect numbers and operation symbols (= - x ÷) on cards or tags (e.g. Tagtiv8 resources[7]) either from each other or from hoops spread around the hall. Children then use these in solving problems involving the four operations.
  - Children walk and run around the school grounds, collecting stimuli (e.g. pictures linked to a history topic, materials for science or art, etc.) to use in the next phase of learning when they are back in the classroom.
  - Children move back and forth in a hall or playground space, collecting questions and answers to a given problem, and then match these

7   See https://tagtiv8.com/active-learning-tagtiv8/.

correctly. This highlights both the current level of understanding and any misconceptions, which the teacher can deal with immediately.

> Children go for a supervised walk around the school grounds or local area to gather data to support their geography investigation on either human or physical features of their local environment.

> The class could go on a treasure hunt together (around the classroom/hall/outdoor space), locating each small step of the new process as they go.

The amount of children that are actually moving will vary depending on the space available and the nature of the activity, but as we continue to say – some movement is better than no movement! This approach is clearly linked to the prestructural, unistructural and multistructural parts of SOLO taxonomy, and our experience in classrooms has shown that by physical collection (often through collaboration with peers), the children will perform much better in the relational and extended abstract phases of their learning. A good example of this is when children are trying to write creatively. Here, they can collect vocabulary/phrases generated by their peers, which have either been posted at 'stations' around the classroom (created by the teacher), or by visiting a set number of different children's/group's current work. This ensures children are proactive explorers in their learning rather than passive recipients of visual prompts provided by the teacher.

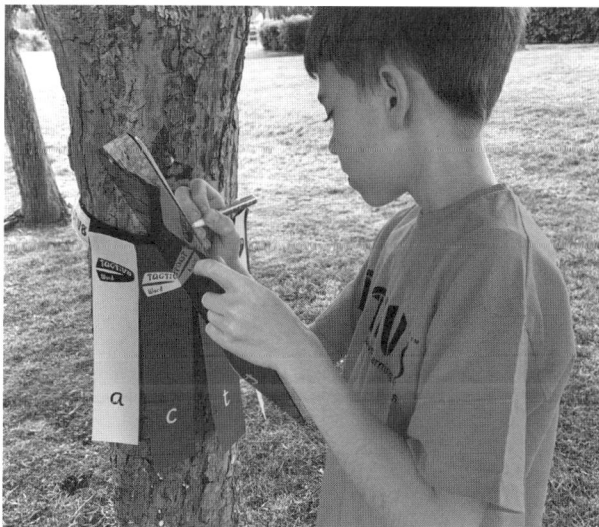

Move & Learn Modelling

Modelling is when a new concept or skill is demonstrated to a learner. This can be done in many different ways (through visual, auditory or kinaesthetic methods) but, regardless of the method, it needs to be done effectively so that children can then use it at relational and extended abstract levels. In considering the use of movement in modelling, the famous quote attributed to Benjamin Franklin comes to mind: 'Tell me and I forget, teach me and I may remember, involve me and I learn.'[8] The Move & Learn Modelling approach features teachers helping and involving children to physically model the concepts of learning they are trying to teach. You could use the children to:

- Represent different points in history, presenting this on a large-scale timeline (you may need a hall, corridor or playground for this!).

- Demonstrate the part-whole model or bar modelling in maths with simple PE equipment (e.g. hoops/chalk for circles and beanbags).

- Demonstrate the relationship of particles in solids, liquids and gases in Key Stage 2 science by thinking about the connections and spaces between them.

- Demonstrate multiplication arrays using the children themselves.

- Demonstrate the need for algorithms and debugging, by getting the children to 'programme' each other from one location to another with sequenced instructions.

- Demonstrate characters' feelings in a book through role play and drama rather than relying on written comprehension questions.

This approach is clearly linked to the prestructural, unistructural and multistructural parts of SOLO taxonomy, as children use themselves as the resources to explore their initial understanding of concepts. While we hope the approaches outlined here make learning more fun and memorable for children when learning new concepts, we also need to stress the importance of ensuring that the learning is semantic (around the knowledge/skill learned) rather than episodic (remembering the experience). This can be reinforced by the class teacher through regular retrieval of the learning over time in different contexts.

8   See https://quoteinvestigator.com/2019/02/27/tell/.

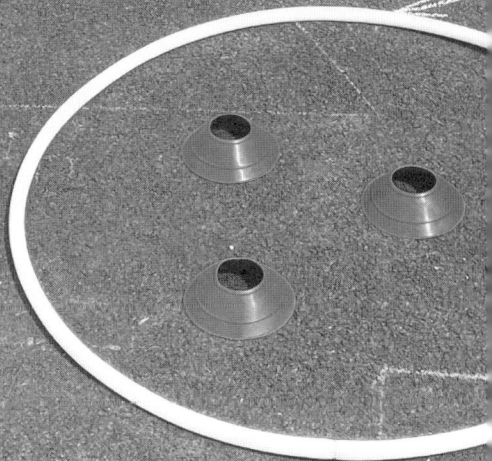

Move & Learn Connection

Making connections in our learning is essential to ensure a greater depth of understanding; this is where the learner moves from the multistructural to the relational aspect of SOLO taxonomy; for example, a child might know various facts about the topic they are studying (e.g. the respiratory system), and be able to explain them individually (e.g. uses oxygen, produces carbon dioxide), but only once they make connections between them (e.g. products of digestion – glucose – react with the oxygen we breathe in to produce carbon dioxide which is breathed out by our lungs, and energy is released) are they moving to the relational level of understanding.

Move & Learn Connection approaches seek to use the children as the individual components of knowledge so that, as they move around and discuss these with their peers through purposeful activities, they can pass on their learning to each other and deepen their understanding. Clearly, there is also the possibility of misconceptions being shared which is why, where possible, we'd recommend either mini plenaries to check for these, or Post-it notes/whiteboard jottings so the teacher can sweep and rectify these immediately; for example, at a multistructural level, a teacher might ask each child to write a word or phrase – linked to a topic they are studying – on a Post-it note, and post this somewhere around the learning environment, looking at other children's ideas too as they do this. They would then (either independently or with peer support) move around again with a notebook or whiteboard to record three ideas that have something in common, structuring them into a connected piece of writing back at their desks – thus beginning movement towards the relational level of understanding. This approach links closely with Kagan structures which promote increased student engagement and cooperation.[9] Our Move & Learn Connection approaches often link closely to these and some of our examples include:

- **Conversation stations:** A teacher posts possible answers to a question around a learning environment. Children move to the answer they think is the best fit and then have to discuss why they chose this with other children that have gone to the same station. One child is then randomly selected by the teacher to give feedback to the class.

9   S. Kagan, Kagan structures, simply put, *Kagan Online* (n.d.). Available at: https://www.kaganonline.com/free_articles/dr_spencer_kagan/ASK38.php.

- **World cafe/Speed learning:** Children in small groups become 'experts' on a particular concept (reading/research material provided by the class teacher). One child then rotates to another group and explains the information. As the lesson progresses, choose different children to rotate, sharing the information as they move.

- **Know, don't know, new to me:** Information is posted around the classroom by a teacher (or potentially students) and children have to move around marking it up as:

  > **:)** (I know/understand this)

  > **?** (I don't understand this)

  > **!** (This is new information to me)

  In groups, the children then talk through **?** and **!** to share and improve their understanding.

- **Seek and you shall find:** On a piece of paper or whiteboard, children write questions (or are given prompts) on something they need support or help with on a specific aspect of learning. They then have to move around the learning environment and find someone that knows the answer(s) and record these on the paper as they go.

- **Find, order, explain:** This involves taking a concept (e.g. column addition, the water cycle) and posting the relevant parts around a learning environment. A group of children then have to find a part each and work together collaboratively to explain to the rest of the class the correct sequence/order, with support from the teacher.

- **Move, pair, share:** Children move around the classroom and when the teacher calls out 'pair', children have to share knowledge/information with a different child.

- **Kagan's inside–outside circle:** Children stand in two concentric circles facing each other and the teacher poses a question for children standing opposite each other to discuss. The teacher then rotates the inner or outer circle and children discuss their answer with another child. The teacher can move the circles in different directions to enable different children to learn from each other. For example, in maths children can share knowledge about properties of shapes – when they come up with another property they are rotated. Alternatively, in English, children can share adjectives to describe a character or a setting.

● **Move, view and review:** Children leave their work open and move around the room to view others' progress either part-way through or towards the end of a learning sequence. They can then use Post-it notes to make constructive comments.

● **Kagan's roving reporter:** Children are given time to either write down what they know or solutions to a problem, before being given permission by the teacher to 'rove' around the classroom for a specific period of time, gathering ideas/answers from other children to support them with their own learning. Notebooks or whiteboards can be taken with children to record ideas/answers, but the key to ensuring learning (rather than copying) is actually taking place here involves effective follow-up questioning by the teacher.

There are many variations of these strategies that can be used to incorporate movement to help children make connections with each other and improve their learning. Different teachers will come up with different ways to make this work for their environments and the children they teach. However, it is all about effective collaboration which, according to Dylan Wiliam, needs two things to be effective: 1) ensuring group goals (activating students as effective instructional resources for each other); and 2) ensuring individual accountability (activating students as own-ers of their own learning).[10] If you ask any teacher, these can be challenging criteria to achieve, which is why group tasks may not be used, particularly when more traditional pedagogical approaches are adopted. However, if the collaborative task is clearly defined by the teacher (small steps!) and every child in the group knows they are accountable for the outcome, then we have seen that this is an extremely effective method for improving both engagement and attainment – for example, if a teacher sends a group of four children to move around a room to collect possible correct answers to a question, it is inevitable that a few children may disengage from the task even though it includes movement. However, if children have to collect just one possible answer each, and then discuss the reason it was collected with their group when they are back at their table, this increases accountability.

10 D. Wiliam, Collaborative learning [video], *Education Scotland* (15 July 2016). Available at: https://youtu.be/TqBNWEQmBRM.

Move & Learn Creation

This final direct-purpose approach links to the final level of SOLO taxonomy – extended abstract. This is where children use movement to make connections beyond the scope of the problem or question, and can transfer learning into new contexts and situations. Examples include children:

- Using their bodies and movement to tell a story they have developed in their English work through dance, mime or by creating a tableau.

- Constructing a pictogram in maths using natural objects.

- Making a bug hotel based on their knowledge of habitats for science.

- Creating art installations or models using natural items collected from the forest area; using their knowledge and understanding from inspirational artists or designers to explore their own styles.

- Creating large-scale maps using chalks on the playground and/or natural items collected from the forest area and/or small items of PE equipment. These maps could demonstrate places visited or locations of biomes around the world.

- Using their knowledge of times tables facts to create different physical representations of arrays, using each other as the representation (e.g. 24 children used to represent 1 x 24, 2 x 12, 3 x 8, 4 x 6 on the playground).

- Combining their knowledge of fundamental movement skills and instructional writing to create their own recipe for how to make a PE lesson both fun and active, with a specific set of resources provided by the teacher.

- Representing coding instructions with body parts and movements to demonstrate simple algorithms.

- Depicting the water cycle with body parts and movements and/or easily accessed natural and/or man-made materials.

- Designing and building large junk model structures to demonstrate their understanding of structures and mechanisms in design and technology.

- Composing and performing a piece of music using body percussion.

Move & Learn Energisers

Energisers (active breaks) recognise that children (particularly younger students) may not effectively learn in traditional 1-hour lesson times, and provide short active breaks (either in the classroom or outside) to allow the brain the chance to recharge at key points within their learning. There is a range of research on children's attention span, which indicates that a child will only be able to maintain focus on a specific task for a few minutes per year of their age.[11] For example, a child starting school at 4 years of age would have an average attention span of 10 minutes. Even by the end of Key Stage 2, the average attention span would still only be approximately 30 minutes.

Of course, how long a child is really able to focus will also be determined by social and behavioural factors including nutrition, sleep, specific learning or behavioural needs, engagement in the activity and environmental distractions. Clearly, for learning to be optimal for a child then these variable factors need to be addressed, but that still doesn't get away from the fact that children in primary schools will only be able to focus on average for between 8 and 30 minutes depending on their age. Therefore, by using physically active breaks more regularly through the school day, children should be able to focus for longer in total. So, at the extreme end of the scale, rather than paying attention for 8 minutes in a 1-hour lesson, children have two 25-minute lessons with a 10-minute active break, and therefore double the time (2 x 8 minutes) they are paying attention for in 1 hour. The timing of when the break takes place, and for how long, is key to ensure this is both purposeful and effective.

Recent research has shown that 'active breaks can effectively reduce sitting and increase standing/stepping and improve on-task behaviour, but the regular implementation of these activities might require time for teachers to become familiar with'.[12] This is why it is so important, as with all routines, that the children need to know the expectations for transition to and from the learning environment (e.g. 'we go and return calmly/silently'), and for the physical activity itself. If this is not the case, then a 10-minute active break can easily become a 20-minute distraction in a lesson – which has stopped, and will stop, teachers using them. There are a wide

---

11 M. Tremolada, L. Taverna and S. Bonichini, Which factors influence attentional functions? Attention assessed by KiTAP in 105 6-to-10-year-old children, *Behavioral Sciences (Basel)* 9(1) (2019): 7.

12 E. Mazzoli, J. Salmon, W-P. Teo, C. Pesce, J. He, T. D. Ben-Soussan et al.., Breaking up classroom sitting time with cognitively engaging physical activity: behavioural and brain responses, *PLoS ONE* 16(7) (2021): e0253733.

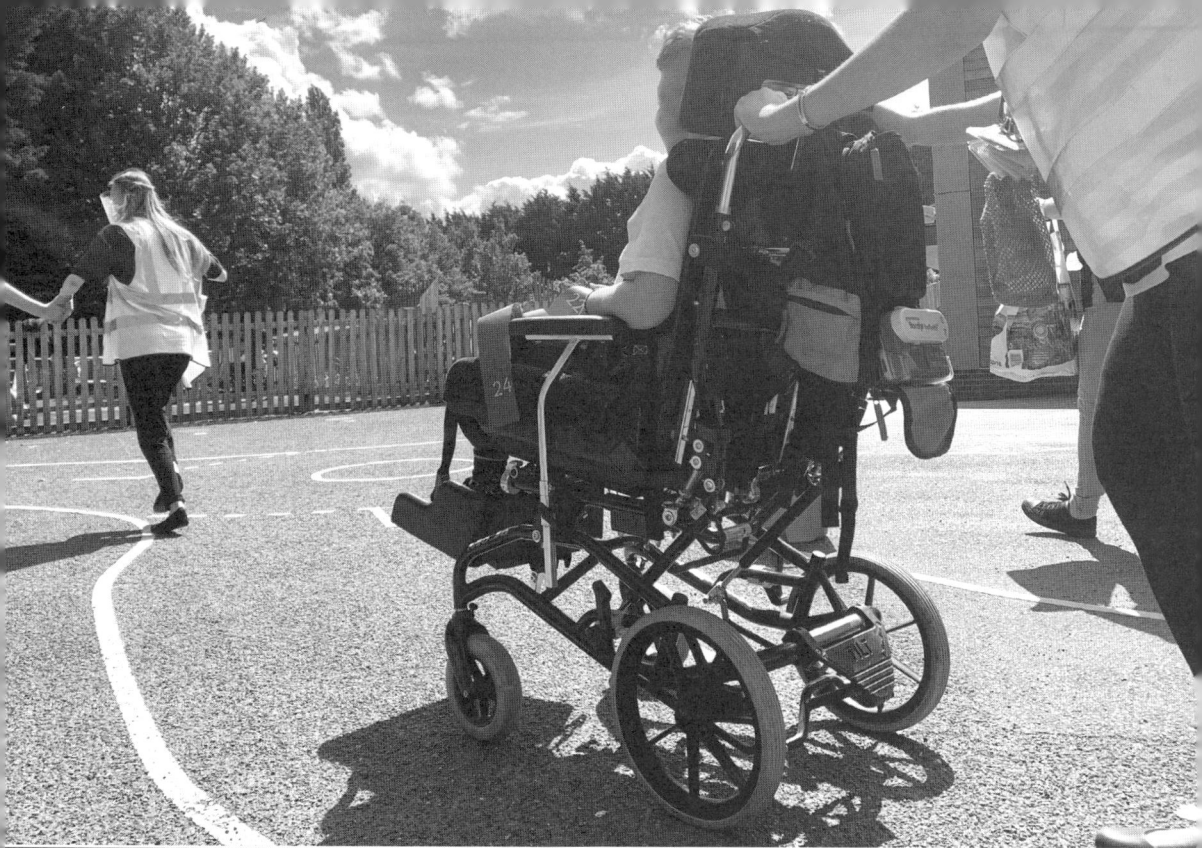

range of free and paid-for resources that can help teachers make these breaks engaging and purposeful for the children, while also supporting them in refocusing the children quickly for the next steps in their learning. Examples include:

- Active walk/jog/run.
- Traditional games, for example tig, hide and seek, follow the leader, hopscotch (need several chalked versions available but children could draw these as part of the break).
- Skipping, hula-hooping (although need equipment for this).
- Yoga/Pilates (including chair/seated versions) – can often be useful for limited space and reducing transition time.
- Online dance/exercise videos – useful for indoors and inclement weather but be careful that, as a teacher, you do not become detached from this process and that all children are able to follow the moves in an enjoyable way.

The key factors that make these active breaks both purposeful and effective for children and teachers (and ensure they are used regularly) are:

- Making the activity enjoyable and engaging for the children. Do not do the same thing every day – you will quickly lose some (if not all) of their engagement unless you offer variety. In addition, following the recent study outlined above, further research is still required to confirm which type of active break best facilitates cognition.
- Involving the children in choosing activities – they are more likely to be motivated to do them.
- Practising them as part of your induction (or even as warm-up activities in PE lessons) so when they need to be used in other lessons, no time is wasted and expectations are clear.

Please note, it is really important that these breaks do not replace unstructured free-play time (e.g. traditional break and lunchtime), as it is still essential that children have this time for their personal, social and emotional development.[13]

---

13 C. L. Ramstetter, R. Murray and A. S. Garner, The crucial role of recess in schools, *Journal of School Health* 80(11) (2010): 517–526.

Setting expectations – behaviour and control

As with any effective classroom strategy, behaviour and expectations are the fundamental grounding to success. This aspect of implementing Move & Learn approaches is a key barrier that teachers will raise. Some may argue that by allowing movement, they will lose control of the class and behaviour will deteriorate as there are too many distractions to the children's learning. Firstly, we absolutely agree that children will not learn if behaviour is not excellent and expectations of achievement are not high. However, if we examine what leads to exemplary behaviour the key factors are:

- Teachers defining the rules/expectations and routines clearly to children.

- Children knowing (and being reminded of) the rules/expectations and routines.

- Teachers applying the rules/expectations and routines consistently.

Seating plans/carpet spaces are often used by teachers to provide this expectation and to allow them to direct their teaching in a targeted way. This allows them to teach and the children to focus/learn. However, this approach will only work if the key factors mentioned are followed, if the teacher is delivering high-quality instruction or teaching methods, and the children are fully engaged in what is going on. We can often have excellent behaviour and well-sequenced teaching, but how do we know that children listening are actually learning anything? What if the teacher had clearly defined to the children the expectations for moving around the classroom during lessons, and consistently reinforced these in every lesson of every day of every week? Children would then know how movement can support their learning and that they are doing it for a purpose. Some ideas for setting expectations in this area could include:

- Movement in our lessons is just another instruction – we need to listen carefully so we know what we are doing and why.

- Movement in our lessons is non-contact.

- We move around our classroom calmly and purposefully.

● Our lessons include movement time and sitting time – both are your opportunities to learn.

If teachers are willing and able to spend the time setting up and reinforcing these expectations, they will not only ensure positive behaviour in their classroom, they will hopefully find that the children are more engaged due to being less sedentary, and no more will the phrase 'they just don't know how to sit still' be uttered!

Purposefully selecting Move & Learn approaches

Having considered how behaviour and expectations can be managed to allow movement to take place in lessons, it is then absolutely vital that teachers select approaches that are purposeful for their learners. Firstly, a teacher needs to consider whether they want to use the movement as an activator or an energiser and how this fits into the sequence of teaching and learning. Without this there is a risk that children will remember the fun movement activity but not the underlying learning. This will also ensure that the reduction in sedentary time is not just for the sake of it, as otherwise it may prove beneficial from a physical activity perspective but not from a learning one. If the movement being used is too complicated for the learner or not actually aligned with the learning, this could lead to cognitive load (where the learner is more focused on how to move and therefore unable to focus on the learning required[14]) or the split-attention effect (the learner is distracted by the movement as it has no real relevance to the learning required[15]). Ultimately, low-level movement to enhance children's learning is better than vigorous movement with no purpose!

As we conclude this chapter, it's worth reflecting on how this section fits into the rest of our CARE model:

● **Culture and ethos:** We need to develop teachers' confidence, motivation and capability in these areas in order to address the perceived barriers and challenges referred to in Chapter 2, and therefore it is vital that small steps

---

14 P. Chandler and J. Sweller, Cognitive load theory and the format of instruction, *Cognition and Instruction* 8(4) (1991): 293–332.
15 P. Chandler and J. Sweller, The split-attention effect as a factor in the design of instruction, *British Journal of Educational Psychology* 62(2) (1992): 233–246.

are taken and teachers do not try all the approaches at once. This is fundamental to establishing and adapting routines so that children know how to behave when they move, as well as when they sit still.

- **Resources:** We believe the best approach to resourcing is teachers adapting their lessons in line with their own and their school's pedagogy, but Chapter 5 also provides some useful resources to support teachers in beginning their Move & Learn journey.

- **Environments:** The level of physical activity you can use will depend on the environment available. Throughout this chapter we have often referred to approaches in the classroom which will usually only lead to low-level movement. With the availability of a hall space, playground or field, these approaches could be used with more MVPA. If movement is used purposefully then the intensity of activity (referred to as low, moderate or vigorous physical activity) is not important and will depend on the nature of the task and the learning environment used for the lesson (the where – see Chapter 5) – for example, in a classroom with 30 children, you would only expect to see LPA, whereas in a playground space the movement incorporated into a lesson may be moderate to vigorous. Ultimately, as highlighted in Chapter 1, any move away from persistent sedentary behaviour is beneficial, and if it is movement for purpose, it is likely to be more engaging and relevant (for both the children and teacher) over time.

Chapter 3	Approaches – Moving along

Questions
& Tasks

1. Consider behaviour expectations and attitudes to learning in your school. Can you redefine these rules/routines/responsibilities to include movement both before, during and after lessons?

2. Ask each teacher in your school to analyse different lessons they have recently taught. How much time do they think was actually spent on effective learning? Share, discuss and consider how the six Move & Learn approaches could be used to adapt future teaching and learning in your setting. Which would be easiest/hardest to implement in your setting and why?

3. Using a range of existing lesson plans (e.g. maths, English, wider curriculum) consider the following:

   a. How could they be adapted to incorporate movement?

   b. Which of the Move & Learn approaches is this?

   c. Can you spot any common themes in relation to when you feel able/willing to incorporate movement into lessons?

   d. Do your colleagues have similar outcomes from doing this task and what can you learn from each other?

small steps
big difference

Based on what you have learned in this chapter, here are six simple ideas to help you begin to use Move & Learn approaches effectively in your practice:

1. Set up a Move & Learn Retrieval activity around a learning space that works for your children and you (e.g. class/hall/outdoor space – why not try all three, one week at a time?).

2. Rather than using a smartboard/PowerPoint stimulus, post visuals around the classroom using a Move & Learn Collection approach. Get the children to investigate in groups – remembering group accountability – and then share their understanding with you and their peers.

3. Try Move & Learn Modelling when teaching a new concept, by using children as the physical resources.

4. Try a Move & Learn Energiser to re-energise/refocus the children and consider which part of the teaching sequence this has supported.

5. Set up a Move & Learn Connection activity part-way through a lesson (to support guided or independent practice), or at the end of the lesson (as an assessment for learning task).

6. Ask the children in your class to come up with three ways they could use movement in their learning, and which subjects would be best suited to this (Move & Learn Creation).

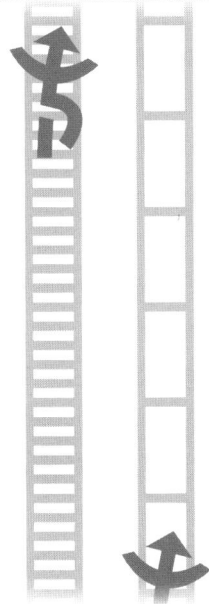

Move & Learn Approaches Across the Pedagogical Spectrum

One reason why Move & Learn approaches have not been adopted by more schools more quickly, particularly in the UK, is that all teachers, schools and governments have their own perspective regarding what good teaching and learning looks like. We refer to this as pedagogy – the art or science (depending on your perspective) of teaching, and the way that the teacher delivers the content of the curriculum to the students. It originates from the Greek word *paidagogos* (child leader). Teachers may use different approaches depending on the age of students, the content being delivered and the research they have read or been trained on. There are wide-ranging pedagogical theories based on research and practice currently used in our education system that are often grouped as follows:

● **Traditional:** Teacher-centred, with an emphasis on knowledge and whole-class instructional modelling and demonstration. Predominantly focuses on the use of textbooks, workbooks, knowledge organisers and quizzes in written form.

- **Progressive:** Child-centred, with more enquiry and play-based approaches (as individuals and with groups) focusing on a development of skills through hands-on experiences in enriching environments with personalised materials.

- **Centrist:** blended approach of traditional and progressive.

We believe that Move & Learn approaches can be incorporated into any of these theories; we will exemplify this by considering the two ends of the pedagogical spectrum.

Move & Learn through play (a progressive approach)

You may well have heard – or even given – these instructions to children: 'Finish your work, then you can go outside to play'; 'You can play after you have finished your work'. What message is this giving to children? That work is more important than play? Is play work's poor relation? Article 31 of the United Nations Convention on the Rights of the Child creates a specific right for all children to have 'rest and leisure, to engage in play and recreational activities appropriate to the age of the child and to participate freely in cultural life and the arts'.[1] Sadly, in the eyes of some parents – as well as other adults and certain sections of the media – teachers of the EYFS aren't real teachers. Even teachers themselves sometimes forget that the basis for all learning starts through play. Maybe all teachers need to ask themselves 'Why should we promote play?' and 'Why is it essential in early childhood experiences?' In the HundrED article 'Why Play is the Answer to Promote Creativity and Joy in Children', Ruth Swailes states: 'Play provides children with opportunities to explore, experiment and make sense of their world, practise skills in a safe space and develop physical, social and emotional skills. Play is essential for all humans.' In the same article, other EYFS practitioners say: 'Open-ended play offers the opportunity for children to become experts – to test, modify or change and

---

1   See https://www.unicef.org/child-rights-convention/convention-text; https://www.childcomwales.org.uk/wp-content/uploads/2018/04/Play-FINAL.pdf.

improve, collaborate, fail and succeed … Play is the way children learn – it's how we open them up to other ideas and encourage curiosity. Play encourages brain development.'[2]

As to the principles of play, Michael Follett recognises that there are 'three simple principles which capture the definitive aspects of play'. Play is:

1   Self-directed.

2   Intrinsically motivated.

3   Freely chosen.[3]

Or, to quote the words of a child from the same book, 'Play is what I do when everyone else has stopped telling me what to do.'[4]

For this chapter we will focus on using Bob Hughes' taxonomy of play, used by Play Scotland,[5] to define 16 types of play:

1   **Symbolic play:** Using objects, actions or ideas to represent other objects, actions or ideas (e.g. using a stick as a magic wand or lightsabre).

2   **Rough and tumble play:** Positive play fighting – gauging relative strength.

3   **Socio-dramatic play:** Play acting (e.g. playing families).

4   **Social play:** Interacting with others, perhaps following a set of rules during a game or while making something together.

5   **Creative play:** Exploring and imagining, trying out new ideas while using different items (e.g. loose-parts junk).

6   **Communication play:** Using facial expressions and body language (e.g. charades).

7   **Dramatic play:** Role playing and acting.

8   **Locomotor play:** Playing for fun (e.g. tag, hide and seek).

---

2   B. Llewellyn and R. Pukhraj, Why play is the answer to promote creativity and joy in children, *HundrED*, (21 March 2020). Available at: https://hundred.org/en/articles/ why-play-is-the-answer-to-promote-creativity-joy-in-children#aee7cf5d.

3   M. Follett, *Creating Excellence in Primary School Playtimes* [Kindle edn] (London: Jessica Kingsley Publishers, 2017), p. 15.

4   Follett, *Creating Excellence*, p. 15.

5   Play Scotland, Play Scotland Play Types Poster (n.d.). Available at: https://www.playscotland.org/resources/ play-types-poster/.

9   **Deep play:** Risk taking and overcoming fears (e.g. obstacle courses).

10   **Exploratory play:** Using the senses to explore and discover the texture environment.

11   **Fantasy play:** Acting out roles that are unlikely to occur (e.g. space explorer).

12   **Imaginative play:** Pretending you can do things beyond normality (e.g. flying like a bird).

13   **Mastery play:** Controlling the physical environment (e.g. digging, building dens).

14   **Object play:** Sequencing fine motor skills (e.g. painting).

15   **Role play:** Exploring ways of being (e.g. pretending to use a mobile phone).

16   **Recapitulative play:** Exploring myths, legends, etc.

Given these definitions of play, it is easy to see how our Move & Learn approaches align with child-centred learning, as they both focus on exploration and social connections. Picture the scene with children in the EYFS learning about plants and growth, some of whom decide to go and play in the soil outside. They go and fetch small trowels, buckets, gardening gloves and watering cans using their prior knowledge of what might help them (Move & Learn Retrieval). From discussions with their teacher and having uncovered some minibeasts while digging, some children go and collect small containers and magnifying glasses (Move & Learn Collection). One of the children is fascinated by the way the minibeasts move and starts mimicking this themselves (Move & Learn Modelling). Following facilitation by the teacher, the other children join in, showing different ways the minibeasts might move. In a different area, some other children have set up their own garden shop role play with books and images of minibeasts. The children who have been digging move to this area and explore and identify with the other children the minibeasts they have seen, sharing what they are, how they move and other information from the books (Move & Learn Connection). In a follow-up session, some children decide to go and perform a play or dance about minibeasts (Move & Learn Creation).

Admittedly, this is a familiar scene in the EYFS, but how can we apply similar principles in a Key Stage 2 environment? Continuing the same theme, the Key Stage 2 children are learning about food chains. The lesson is introduced through a game or quiz to discover what the children know already, with children given four choices for each question and moving to the appropriate corner of the room depending on the answer (Move & Learn Retrieval). The children are then provided with a range of resources (books, fact files) spread around the learning environment and they go and choose which ones they wish to use to support their learning (Move & Learn Collection). The children then play a game in the hall or outside space, facilitated by the teacher, with children given different bibs to represent different animals or plants; they can only tag the animal or plant they would consume in their part of the food chain (Move & Learn Modelling). In groups, children are then allowed to choose a project to do with what they have learned about food chains, resulting in some children making their own videos, while others use drama and dance to illustrate – through movement – how their food chain works (Move & Learn Connection and Creation). We recognise that the group element of this would be dependent on the space and the availability of supporting adults.

Clearly, the two examples provided here involve every Move & Learn strategy in the learning process, which will not normally be the case. However, we wanted to illustrate in relation to play pedagogy how powerful Move & Learn can be.

Move & Learn through instruction (a traditional approach)

From the outside, we have no doubt that many practitioners would probably align our Move & Learn strategies with a progressive approach. However, we believe Move & Learn can also be effectively incorporated into a traditional approach – and, therefore, anywhere in between on the pedagogical spectrum. We will use Rosenshine's principles of instruction,[6] which are widely used in practice and highly respected in the ResearchED community,[7] to outline how our Move & Learn approaches can be purposefully implemented in this way. Rosenshine highlighted 10 key principles which focus upon the key things teachers do through their instruction to enable high-quality learning outcomes. We will now outline how you can incorporate Move & Learn strategies purposefully within these principles to maximise the outcomes of your instruction.

---

6   B. Rosenshine, Principles of instruction: research-based strategies that all teachers should know, *American Educator* 36(1) (2012): 12–19.

7   See https://researched.org.uk.

1   **Begin a lesson with a short review of previous learning: daily review can strengthen previous learning and lead to fluent recall**

This is important because our working memory is limited, and therefore if we do not do this short review, children have to work harder to recall old material while trying to learn something new. This links to our Move & Learn Retrieval approach (see page 38).

2   **Present new material in small steps with student practice after each step: only present small amounts of new material at any time, and then assist students as they practice this material**

The key to successful teaching here is that the teachers do not overwhelm their students by presenting too much new material at once, and also ensure that they have mastered it before the next point is introduced. An effective example, used in Rosenshine's paper, is of a teacher that taught a strategy for summarising a paragraph in small steps. Firstly, the teacher modelled and thought aloud as she identified the topic of a paragraph; then she led practice on identifying the topics of new paragraphs; then she taught students to identify the main idea of a paragraph. The teacher modelled this step and then supervised the students as they practised both finding the topic and locating the main idea. Following this, the teacher taught the students to identify supporting details in a paragraph. The teacher modelled and thought aloud, and then the students practised. Finally, the students practised carrying out all three steps of this strategy. This means the strategy was divided into smaller steps and there was modelling and practice at each step. From a Move & Learn perspective, new material can be delivered in small steps using:

> **Move & Learn Collection (see page 41):** Using the example provided by Rosenshine, this can be used when the teacher is leading the practice of identifying the topics of new paragraphs, or locating the main idea. Incidentally, the reference to movement is not lost on us. An example of how this could be achieved through movement is by posting both correct and incorrect answers around the learning environment. As a group or groups of children search, locate and select these, the current level of understanding is highlighted but also any potential misconceptions which the teacher can then deal with immediately.

> **Move & Learn Energisers (see page 52):** Using active breaks to break the learning down into smaller steps for the children, but also to recognise the impact physical activity has on our brain – particularly in relation to our mindset, learning and memory.[8]

3 **Ask a large number of questions and check the responses of all students: questions help students practice new information and connect new material to their prior learning**

Rosenshine states: 'questions allow a teacher to determine how well the material has been learned and the need for additional instruction. The most effective teachers also ask students to explain the process they used to answer the question.'[9] A key part in ensuring that questions are effective is checking the responses of *all* students. Examples given by Rosenshine of how this was achieved by imaginative teachers include:

> Tell the answer to a neighbour.

> Summarise the main idea in one or two sentences, writing the summary on a piece of paper and sharing this with a neighbour, or repeating the procedures with a neighbour.

> Write the answer on a card and then hold it up.

> Raise their hands if they know the answer (thereby allowing the teacher to check the entire class).

> Raise their hands if they agree with the answer that someone else has given.

We can easily apply Move & Learn principles to these ideas by utilising light-intensity Move & Learn Connection approaches:

> **Tell the answer to a neighbour:** A particularly good strategy for this idea is for children to discuss a question or a problem with a small group and then one person remains behind to be the 'expert' as all the groups move around. If you make a different child remain at the table each time, then you increase student accountability.

> **Summarise the main idea in one or two sentences, writing the summary or procedure on a piece of paper:** Children then move in an

---

8 Ratey and Hagerman, *Spark!*, p. 24.
9 Rosenshine, Principles, p. 14.

ordered way around the classroom, reviewing up to three different answers and possibly adding their own responses if appropriate/desired.

> **Write the answer on a card and then hold it up:** Some children move to cards posted at various points around the learning environment and write the answer on a card. They then take this to the front of the class and hold it up to share with the teacher and their peers.

> **Raise their hands if they know the answer:** Stand up/move to a specific part of the room (if using multiple choice) if they know the answer, thereby allowing the teacher to check the entire class. There is always a risk children will just follow their peers – this will either mean they then know the right answer (and didn't before) and/or the teacher notices they follow and then addresses through questioning or one-to-one support.

> **Raise their hands if they agree with the answer that someone else has given:** Stand up/move to a specific part of the room if they agree.

Rosenshine then states that the purpose of all these procedures is to provide 'active participation' for the students and also allow the teacher to see how many students are correct and confident. This ties in perfectly with our Move & Learn principles of making learning more engaging and actively involving all students (in the most literal sense). He even refers to teachers using choral responses to make the practice seem more like a game (note – this is only effective when all students start together). A really simple Move & Learn example of this can be seen when practising times tables in maths; in such cases, children can use different body shapes or patterns (e.g. star jump for four, high five for five) to support them in answering these questions.

4   **Provide models: providing students with models and worked examples can help them learn to solve problems faster**

The best way to summarise this is that 'many of the skills taught in classrooms can be conveyed by providing prompts, modelling use of the prompt, and then guiding students as they develop independence'.[10] This ultimately involves using a worked example, or in specific subjects in the primary sector, a WAGOLL (what a good one looks like). This supports

....

10 Rosenshine, Principles, p. 15.

children as they move from i) a *teacher does* (teacher models a complete problem, talking it through and checking understanding as they go), to ii) a collective *we do* (where the students work through another model or series of models guided by the teacher), to iii) an individual *I can do* way of working (where children are able to work on further problems independently).[11]

From a Move & Learn perspective, there are two huge opportunities here:

›   **Move & Learn Collection:** Children collect new vocabulary (e.g. adverbs) from around the room, for example, which the teacher then uses to model in sentences as worked examples before independent practice.

›   **Move & Learn Modelling:** Use the children and chalk/hoops to demonstrate a part-part-whole model in maths, for example.

These two approaches will make the learning more fun and memorable (but in a way that is linked to the learning, rather than the experience provided), which ensures children still learn these new concepts in an effective way.

5   **Guide student practice: successful teachers spend more time guiding students' practice of new material**

If we assume that a teacher has used the children as the physical model to explain a new concept – for example, the part-whole model in maths – it is then vital (according to Rosenshine and the research) that they guide student practice through involving them in further worked examples, ensuring a deeper understanding before expecting them to work independently. The key word here is *guide* (another movement word). At this point, a teacher could use Move & Learn Modelling approaches (see page 44), but with smaller groups of children that need the additional support. This will then ensure they are able to navigate their way through the tasks set for independent practice or, as Rosenshine puts it, 'seatwork'![12] At this point, it is worth mentioning that having involved children in movement to model a new concept and the further worked examples, seatwork may well be the most effective method of children demonstrating their knowledge independently, and also allow the teacher to work with smaller groups on more interactive tasks too!

---

11 T. Sherrington, The art of modelling … it's all in the handover, *Teacherhead* (November 2020). Available at: https://teacherhead.com/2020/11/28/the-art-of-modelling-its-all-in-the-handover/.
12 Rosenshine, Principles, p. 16.

6 **Check for student understanding: checking for student understanding at each point can help students learn the material with fewer errors**

The research has shown that checking for understanding has two key purposes: 'a) answering the question might cause the students to elaborate on material they have learned and augment connections to other learning in their long-term memory; and b) alerting the teacher to when parts of the material need to be retaught.'[13]

This is where movement through Move & Learn Connection approaches can be particularly effective, as it not only enables the teacher to check understanding, but for the children to support each other in making the augmented connections or correcting their understanding – for example, either part-way through, or on completion of independent written practice, children could move around the classroom reading three other students' work. The teacher then uses questioning of the individual (through sweeping the environment) and then the class as a whole (when they return to their work) to explore elements of success and feedback for individuals (and the class as a whole) on things to improve or correct. A range of examples have already been shared on page 43, but it is just as important with this stage to ensure that *all* students' understanding is checked by the teacher, and that if the collaborative tasks are used, the group goals and individual accountability are again clearly defined by the teacher.

If appropriate to the learning content, the Move & Learn Retrieval approach (see page 38) could also be used (e.g. using different body shapes to link to different possible answers; moving to different parts of the room to give a specific answer or opinion). Once the teacher has checked and ascertained the level of student understanding, they may decide (based on their experience with their children) that a Move & Learn Energiser (see page 52) is necessary to enable children to return to their work as more effective learners – which leads us nicely on to:

---

13 Rosenshine, Principles, p. 16.

7   **Obtain a high success rate: it is important for students to achieve a high success rate during classroom instruction**

'If the practice does not have a high success rate there is a chance that students are practising and learning errors.'[14] Rosenshine refers to an example in his research where he observed an effective teacher that was going from desk to desk during independent practice and suddenly realised that almost all the students were having difficulty. What did she do? She stopped the lesson and retaught it the next day as she did not want the students to practice errors. So, what if we knew of a strategy that might enable this teacher to not have to wait until the next day to return to this concept? What if we knew of a strategy that would help the brain recover from stress and cognitive load? What if the teacher at this point in the lesson decided to take a Move & Learn Energiser? Not only would this be beneficial to the children, but it may also be beneficial to the teacher in reshaping their thinking on how to teach the concept to enhance student understanding.

8   **Provide scaffolds for difficult tasks: the teacher provides students with temporary supports and scaffolds to assist them when they learn difficult tasks**

Scaffolds to support learning can come in many different forms, including:

> Teacher support.

> Peer support – requires teachers to be confident that they are sharing the correct knowledge!

> Visual toolkits.

> Worked examples – including some with errors/misconceptions that students correct.

> Starting prompts/stimulus (e.g. first paragraph modelled effectively as a starting point).

> Checklists/answers to evaluate completed work.

We can use our Move & Learn Collection strategy as the scaffold to support the children's thinking; information could be posted around the learning environment for the children to collect and refer to either before, during or

14 Rosenshine, Principles, p. 17.

after they have completed the work. In terms of utilising teacher or peer support, this could also involve movement – the teacher could move around the learning stations with those children that need a specific scaffold, or specified children could be asked to move to a different table to share their excellent thinking/worked example with children who would benefit from it. Imagine creating a culture in your classroom where being moved to a different desk was not a bad thing!

9 **Require and monitor independent practice: students need extensive, successful, independent practice in order for skills and knowledge to become automatic**

The key here is that any independent practice that students are asked to do is linked to the guided practice that has taken place, so that they can achieve the 'high success rate' previously referred to. Rosenshine states that 'students need to be fully prepared for their independent practice' and 'students were more engaged when the teacher circulated around the room, and monitored and supervised their seatwork'.[15] From a Move & Learn perspective, if movement has already been purposefully linked in the prior areas of the teaching sequence, it may well be that the best form of independent practice is 'seatwork'! This is likely to be the case if the method of independent practice is a traditional written task (e.g. pen/pencil and paper). However, depending on the progress of the students through a lesson, it may be useful to prepare them by offering a Move & Learn Energiser (see page 52) before commencing the task, if this is appropriate. An assumption here is that the independent practice will always be a written task. However, with the right staffing ratios and availability of resources, there are plenty of Move & Learn Modelling (see page 44) and Creation (see page 50) methods that teachers could use. This is seen regularly in the EYFS (e.g. ordering large digit cards in maths on a washing line, writing large letters in the sand or in chalk on the playground), but can be equally effective throughout Key Stage 2 and beyond. In some ways these practical tasks are easier to prepare for and deliver with older children as they should have a higher degree of independence. They may initially take longer to prepare than a traditional independent written or recorded task, but if teachers are willing to take small steps and develop their practice in this

15 Rosenshine, Principles, p. 18.

way, the research (as highlighted in Chapter 2) has again shown that outcomes for children improve. Ultimately, not everything needs to be recorded and written down to be learned!

Rosenshine also refers to the use of cooperative learning, during which students help each other as they study. He refers to the fact that students achieve more in these settings, presumably from either having to explain the material to someone else or having it explained to them by someone other than their teacher. 'Cooperative learning offers an opportunity for students to get feedback from their peers about correct as well as incorrect responses, which promotes both engagement and learning'.[16] Add movement to this type of learning and we get our Move & Learn Connection approach (see page 46), and an example of its use here could be the teacher giving the children a specified amount of time (say, 15 minutes) to undertake independent practice, and then half of an agreed number of children rotate places and share their understanding with others. If the teacher has performed an effective sweep of children's work during this time, they could strategically move children to support those most in need. After five minutes of knowledge sharing, the children could continue with their independent practice followed by further rotation(s) if appropriate.

10 **Engage students in weekly and monthly review: students need to be involved in extensive practice in order to develop well-connected and automatic knowledge**

This is all to do with the fact that the more we review and connect our learning in our long-term memory, we free up capacity in our limited working memory for new information to be processed and for problem solving. Many teachers now operate this review using memory quadrants, where they review the specific learning in a given subject (or a variation of this depending on the age of the children) from last lesson, last week, last term and last year. Move & Learn memory quadrants can be created in the four corners of a classroom, or in larger spaces using tape, chalk or cones. Different children can then be asked to move to the different quadrants (starting with the most recent) to either verbally share their learning (Move & Learn Connection) or retrieve the key concept from somewhere in the

----

16 Rosenshine, *Principles*, p. 19.

learning environment and place it in the correct quadrant (Move & Learn Retrieval).

As you can see, we have come full circle in the teaching and learning cycle, and therefore can link back to the Move & Learn strategies referred to in the first Rosenshine principle as they focus on the retrieval of knowledge from working memory. We have summarised here how each of the Move & Learn approaches align with the different aspects of Rosenshine's principles of instruction to facilitate their use by practitioners:

	Rosenshine									
	1	2	3	4	5	6	7	8	9	10
M&L Retrieval (see page 38)										
M&L Collection (see page 41)										
M&L Modelling (see page 44)										
M&L Connection (see page 46)										
M&L Creation (see page 50)										
M&L Energisers (see page 52)										

Chapter 4	Move & Learn Across the Pedagogical Spectrum – Moving along

Questions
& Tasks

1. Define the pedagogical/teaching and learning approach taken by your school with colleagues. Then consider the following:

    a. How can the six Move & Learn approaches can be incorporated into the pedagogical approach/teaching and learning policy used in your school?

    b. Which approaches would be easiest to implement and have the most impact?

small steps
big difference

We've relisted the **small steps, big difference** ideas from Chapter 3 below. Based on what you have learned in Chapter 4, which ones will now make a difference for the children in your school?

Here are six simple ideas to help you begin to use Move & Learn approaches effectively in your practice:

1. Set up a Move & Learn Retrieval activity around a learning space that works for your children and you (e.g. class/hall/outdoor space – why not try all three, one week at a time?).

2. Rather than using a smartboard/PowerPoint stimulus, post visuals around the classroom using a Move & Learn Collection approach. Get the children to investigate in groups – remembering group accountability – and then share their understanding with you and their peers.

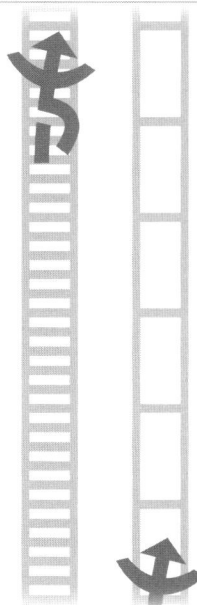

3. Try Move & Learn Modelling when teaching a new concept, by using children as the physical resources.

4. Try a Move & Learn Energiser to re-energise/refocus the children and consider which part of the teaching sequence this has supported.

5. Set up a Move & Learn Connection activity part-way through a lesson (to support guided or independent practice), or at the end of the lesson (as an assessment for learning task).

6. Ask the children in your class to come up with three ways they could use movement in their learning, and which subjects would be best suited to this (Move & Learn Creation).

Chapter 5

Move & Learn Environments and Resources

How do environments shape behaviours?

'Environments' is an oft-used term in education, by researchers and consultants alike. Most teachers, however, refer to them as classrooms. In this chapter, we challenge the assumption that learning can only take place sitting down in a classroom, facing the teacher, often assisted by a whiteboard or smartboard. It could be argued that the Move & Learn ideas proposed in the previous chapter are challenging to implement in the many undersized, overpopulated and poorly designed classrooms that teachers teach in and children learn in. However, even within these limitations and constraints, we feel there are still opportunities to reimagine the places and spaces in which our children learn – both indoors and outdoors. We like to consider the places as the classrooms, the hall and the playground. The spaces are the corridors and other channels that connect the places. Meanwhile, it's the faces – the adults and children – who inhabit the places and spaces, who are central to the learning. By connecting all three 'aces', learning can be even more purposeful, engaging and rewarding in terms of both enjoyment and attainment. Clearly, the intensity of the physical activity – whether it be light, moderate or vigorous – and type of movement linked to learning will not only depend on the purpose of the lesson but also, fundamentally, the space available. Move & Learn strategies in a small classroom with 30 children will only ever involve low levels of physical activity, whereas once a hall or outdoor space is used then moving and learning can easily facilitate moderate-to-vigorous levels. As with any learning activity in any space, a teacher will need to assess how to use the environment most effectively for their learners (including any health and safety considerations), and in doing so should consider the following:

Environments drive behaviours

The psychologist Kurt Lewin's research demonstrates that behaviour is a function of the person and their environment.[1] Therefore, if we think about a child entering a classroom 'to learn', their behaviour – both social and learning – will be dictated not only by themselves, but by the environment that surrounds them. This is not only true of the classroom, but the wider school environment too, which was recognised by Henry Dorling, senior lecturer in sport development and coaching at Solent University, in a UKEDChat article: 'The school environment has been identified more importantly as the arena where habits can be changed and opportunities exploited. Schools can represent a primary socialising influence that has an enormous impact on the course of people's lives and on society. This rings true with all the current information regarding early physical activity interventions and the impact they have on later life … Indeed, the physical environment of the school has been shown to be highly conducive for children to become further engaged with physical activity, which they are less likely to do outside the school influence. The *Designed to Move* report (2012) indicates that the school environment is accessible, and provides an undoubted opportunity for regular, structured play, physical education, physical activity and sports. Additionally, as a spin-off from physical

---

1   K. Lewin, Behavior and development as a function of the total situation. In L. Carmichael (ed.), *Manual of Child Psychology* (New York: John Wiley & Sons Inc., 1946), pp. 791–844.

activity influences, school-based interventions can also affect positive social and environmental problems by developing responsible citizens.'[2]

As Sir Ken Robinson points out, 'A physical environment is more than cosmetic, it affects the mood, motivation, and vitality of the whole school community.'[3] Historically, our classrooms have largely been designed to control the children we teach and ensure calm and purposeful learning places. Huge advances have been made in technology and other areas of life, yet classrooms in Victorian times and now are still remarkably similar, with children sitting in manageable rows or groups. By their very set up, this creates an active–passive relationship, with the teacher moving and the children sitting. Classrooms may be controlled and calm, but we would question whether the learning is truly purposeful for all the children involved. If teachers and schools are willing to invest in Move & Learn approaches, they need to consider how to adapt these environments so that movement takes place naturally as part of the children's learning. It can still be controlled (though we would refer to this as guided) and calm but with more purpose. There are many examples of how people have adapted environments to facilitate more movement. Copenhagen transformed its infrastructure so that more people cycled around the city, with one resident stating, 'I take the bike because it is easier – a function of the environment created to make it so!'[4] If a city can change, surely it is easier to do so within a school. This has been recognised by Lene Jensby Lange, founder of Autens, who works with teachers and students on co-constructing learning environments:[5] 'We need to get so many more tactile resources and invitations to move out there. Textbooks should be Plan B and engaging physically with the world should be the default setting.'[6]

2   H. Dorling, The importance of the school environment, *UKEDChat* (2014). Available at: https://ukedchat. com/2019/04/30/school-environment/; L. MacCallum, N. Howson and N. Gopu, *Designed to Move: A Physical Activity Action Agenda*, Nike (2012). Available at: https://www.sportsthinktank.com/uploads/ designed-to-move-full-report-13.pdf.
3   Ken Robinson and Kate Robinson, *Imagine If ... Creating a Future for Us All* [Kindle edn] (London: Penguin, 2022), p. 77.
4   R. Barton, On your bike: what the world can learn about cycling from Copenhagen, *The Independent* (18 October 2009). Available at: https://www.independent.co.uk/life-style/health-and-families/features/ on-your-bike-what-the-world-can-learn-about-cycling-from-copenhagen-1803227.html.
5   See https://www.autens.dk/en/category/about-learning-spaces/.
6   Personal correspondence.

The teaching and expected learning should dictate the classroom layout, rather than the layout dictating the learning

This was highlighted in the 2016 Teaching Schools Council report *Effective Primary Teaching Practice.* Too often the layout dictates children's learning, whereas 'effective classroom environments focus on pupil learning, providing reference points and scaffolds to support this'.[7] The report went on to state that from the best practice they had seen, effective schools make the most of the classroom environment by considering:

- Having tidy, organised classrooms which, viewed from a pupil's perspective, avoid clutter and unnecessary distraction.

- How the classroom promotes a calm and purposeful approach to learning, helping pupils to focus and supporting pupil's self-regulation.

- How the classroom walls and display enhance, not distract from, teaching and pupil's learning.

- Having resources … available to pupils so that they do not need help to get them.

- Making sure everyone has access to prompts and learning cues to strengthen independence and help pupils move on when they get stuck.[8]

With these in mind, we can consider the different places and spaces where Move & Learn approaches might be used most effectively to support and enhance teaching and learning.

---

7   Teaching Schools Council, *Effective Primary Teaching Practice Report* (2016), p. 32. Available at: http://tactyc.org.uk/wp-content/uploads/2016/08/Effective-primary-teaching-practice-2016-report-web.pdf.
8   Teaching Schools Council, *Effective Primary Teaching*, p. 33.

Activating environments purposefully – where can Move & Learn be used to support and enhance learning?

Classroom

As the environment needs to be flexible to the learners' needs, where practical it should be changed and adapted to ensure the best possible outcomes for students. If we consider the Teaching School Council's criteria from a Move & Learn perspective, we can explore how to integrate purposeful movement into the classroom environment:

- **Tidy, organised classrooms:** Clearly, the less clutter in a classroom, the more space there is to Move & Learn! While children moving might be classed by some as an unnecessary distraction, provided the purpose of the movement has been made clear and it is a part of the learning process (see Chapter 3) then this shouldn't be the case. Our recommendation to start with here is to ensure that the only furniture and resources in the classroom environment are ones that will be used for the children's learning. Many teachers are renowned for their abilities to hoard resources – maybe now is a good time to declutter and/or detox! We often recommend that teachers visit their classrooms during their planning, preparation and assessment (PPA) time, taking pictures of the children – following the school's safeguarding protocol and guidelines – in their environment, and then challenging themselves over whether everything present is actually needed and also what else could be changed to enhance teaching and learning for all.

- **A calm and purposeful approach to learning:** This is where we need to debunk the theory that children can't move around a classroom in a calm and purposeful manner. If movement is part of their routine (see Chapter 3) and they have clear and agreed expectations around this, then movement can actually make their learning more purposeful. So, when they are being asked to retrieve knowledge from memory, they can actually move to collect the words they know posted around the room (Move & Learn Collection approach). Alternatively, when they are trying to learn about place value they can actually come and be part of the model (Move & Learn Modelling approach). The calm is achieved through shared expectations, and the purpose is made more relevant through movement. By allowing a balance of movement and sitting (for independent practice, e.g. writing or reflection) we will also help develop children's self-regulation for different tasks.

- **Displays that enhance children's learning:** Move & Learn Retrieval and Move & Learn Collection approaches in a classroom will often involve children moving slowly around the classroom retrieving/collecting key information to support their learning; for example, this could involve picking up physical resources (e.g. number or word cards) or making notes on the contents of the displays. This means that this information displayed around the classroom is relevant and purposeful for them, and clearly supports and enhances their learning, rather than being seen as wallpaper.

- **Resources that are available to students so that they do not need help to get them:** This links closely to the previous point; Move & Learn approaches enable children to collect and connect ideas from both resources around them but, crucially, from their peers too. By ensuring calm and purposeful movement, children will also benefit from Move & Learn Connection approaches; for example, moving around the classroom to gather ideas from three other children's written work before returning to their own. This was perfectly demonstrated during a lesson led by a Year 5 teacher in a Yorkshire school. With the instruction 'The room is yours to roam', the children left their chairs, armed with jotters or clipboards. The aim was to gather information from images displayed on the walls of the classroom. As one of the boys explained, 'It's better because you can walk and talk and share ideas.' His friend backed up this view: 'If you're sitting next to the same person, you only get to hear their opinions. This way you get more ideas.'

- **Access to prompts and learning cues to strengthen independence and help students move on when they get stuck:** This links to both the previous points as, by adopting Move & Learn approaches, the children know they can visit the maths display to see a worked example for one of the types of questions they are stuck on (Move & Learn Collection approach), or share an explanation linked to a science investigation mid-way through a lesson with a peer from another part of the classroom (Move & Learn Connection approach). These are just two examples that help students 'move on'.

Learning from the EYFS

If you want to look at an environment that meets the key criteria for purposeful learning while also facilitating movement, you need to look no further than a high-quality EYFS setting.[9] Outstanding environments in the EYFS are flexible and make the best use of space. They are collaborative, interactive and develop positive relationships. Fundamentally, they allow children freedom to explore, move, learn and play! So why do we create places that contradict this for children from the age of 6, and then wonder why many of them are not making the academic progress 'required of them' and are finding it challenging to manage personal, social and emotional issues? Children in the EYFS are going through different developmental milestones, but where does research tell us that sitting a child over 6 years old at a desk for four hours a day is optimum for their well-being, personal development and academic attainment? As to the importance of the environment in the EYFS, it is no surprise that the environment is regarded as the third teacher in Reggio Emilia settings[10] – the teacher being the primary teacher and the children the second teachers. The environment is a space for providing numerous opportunities for children to explore, experiment, develop their ideas and test their theories. Much like the Montessori and Steiner approaches,[11] great care is taken to construct an environment that allows for the easy exploration of various interests. We are not saying that all classes should now have sand and water trays, but maybe we can take the lead from pioneering practitioners in Key Stages 1 and 2 in the UK (5–11-year-olds) who have adapted their classrooms to facilitate low-level movement. Standing desks – either purpose built or makeshift – are used to create research areas for small groups of children. Whiteboards as part of displays at children's level support collaborative knowledge sharing, while a balance-ball area provides opportunities for small group work/collaborative learning. Resource examples can be found later in this chapter under 'Bespoke resources' (see page 95).

---

9   Oxfordshire County Council, Oxfordshire Early Years Development & Childcare Partnership and SureStart, *My Space: Creating Enabling Environments for Young Children* (n.d.). Available at: https://www2.oxfordshire. gov.uk/cms/sites/default/files/folders/documents/childreneducationandfamilies/ informationforchildcareproviders/Toolkit/My_Space_Creating_enabling_environments_for_young_ children.pdf.

10 M. A. Biermeier, Inspired by Reggio Emilia: emergent curriculum in relationship-driven learning environments, *NAEYC* (November 2015). Available at: https://www.naeyc.org/resources/pubs/yc/nov2015/ emergent-curriculum.

11 See https://www.steinerwaldorf.org/steiner-education/what-is-steiner-education/; https://montessori-nw. org/about-montessori-education.

Places and spaces – learning on tour

So, we know that environments will impact on behaviour (both social and learning) and that they need to be flexible to learners needs, but what practical steps can practitioners take to activate their classrooms (and extended learning environments) so that movement becomes a natural by-product of a well-designed learning environment and high-quality teaching and learning approaches? As noted previously, we appreciate that traditional classrooms – with the exception of energisers or activators that use 'active videos' (e.g. Go Noodle, BBC Super Movers[12]) – will only ever be able to facilitate low-level movement until there is a radical rethink on how we design the buildings in the first place! Until then, let's consider the benefits of BBC Super Movers with a study involving more than 1,000 schoolchildren. Researchers from Loughborough University looked at the impact of physical activity on behaviour and classroom achievement among primary children from 17 schools across the UK. According to Professor Eef Horgervorst, 'The study showed that the Super Movers programme improved brain speed – up to an average of 19% – and mood, from *okay* to *feeling very good*, significantly in children.'[13]

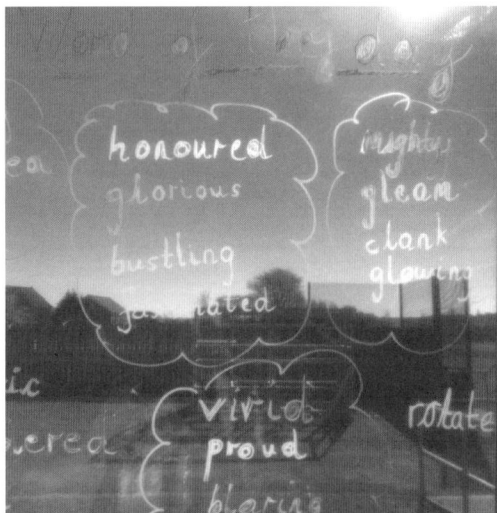

---

12 See https://www.gonoodle.com; https://www.bbc.co.uk/teach/supermovers.
13 Loughborough University, Super Movers: schoolchildren performed better in tests after exercise initiative from the Premier League and BBC (7 March 2019). Available at: https://www.lboro.ac.uk/news-events/news/2019/march/super-movers-brain-power-boost-bbc-premier-league/.

However, it's beyond the classroom where the opportunities for Move & Learn reach their full potential. We accept that the ideal places for Move & Learn to happen are where there is plenty of room to move safely – therefore, hall spaces and the outdoors (playground, field, forest-school area, beyond the school gates) are ideal. But before we get on to these, there are even opportunities to move and learn in the spaces between the places, as we step from the classroom to the corridor. Social media throws up many images of corridors and staircases with markings for children to embed their understanding of multiplication and times tables. A particularly imaginative way to embed trigonometry involves a protractor drawn on the floor where the door opens. The corridor is also an ideal place (if you can't get too far beyond the classroom) for activities such as ordering (in maths) and exploring chronology through timelines (in history). Clearly supervision, safety and high expectations are fundamental to success in these types of activities but, then again, these factors are crucial when teaching and learning in any space. The opportunities for both enhanced learning, engagement and more movement in using places and spaces beyond the classroom are immense and, in planning in the use of these spaces, it is key not only to address supervision, safety and high expectations, but again involve the children in this process so it becomes a routine part of the way they learn. Some schools routinely involve children in book scrutinies and learning walks, so why not get their thoughts on risk assessments? They see matters through different lenses and they will often notice things that adults fail to see. From student voice to student action!

Move & Learn in a hall

The advantages of taking Move & Learn into a hall space is that you have more opportunities to move for all children and do not have to worry about the elements (rain, wind, snow, etc.). In our experience, many primary school halls are invariably unused for large parts of the morning; therefore, this is a great opportunity to take the learning to this larger space. As with all learning outside the classroom, it's important that you have considered how to use the space effectively and how you ensure the children know how to behave in this environment. Similar to an effective PE lesson, this is achieved by assessing the risks with the children, outlining the expectations clearly, and ensuring the children are focused and can hear/see you when you need to give instruction – for example, using a semi-circular coned-off space of the hall to gather them together for this, seated or standing. There are many simple but effective strategies used by schools to optimise the use of the hall for Move & Learn, such as:

- Installing whiteboards on the walls at various places around the hall.

- Including Move & Learn on their whole-school hall timetable.

In respect of the latter, schools could consider ways to use this space for whole classes and smaller targeted groups. And yes, there may well be restrictions around certain times of the day – when setting up for lunch – or over the year as classes prepare for religious celebrations and end-of-year performances. However, if schools prioritise Move & Learn, logistical problems can be overcome. The opportunities for Move & Learn in the hall are endless – whether they utilise LPA or MVPA.

- **Examples of LPA:** Children seek numbers on the floor that are multiples of X or Y (Move & Learn Retrieval). Working in pairs or small groups (Move & Learn Connection), they discuss the numbers they are looking for and return them to their Home Zone. Here, they may be asked to order them, before identifying the missing numbers in the sequence. Likewise, children could seek pairs of numbers to make number bonds of 10, 20 or 100. Alternatively, previous SAT papers could be cut up and the questions spread on the floor or maybe stuck to the walls. Pairs or small groups of children then go from one question to another, discussing possible answers and offering reasons for their answers (Move & Learn Connection).

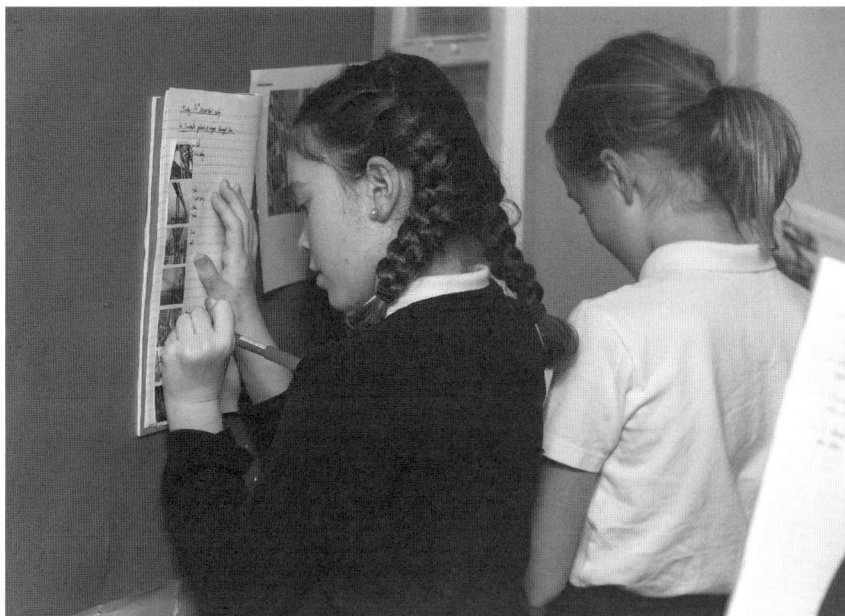

- **Examples of MVPA:** Children run relays to gather numbers from hoops on the floor (Move & Learn Collection). They then complete a series of Thinking Challenges related to the mathematical areas they are studying in the classroom. With younger children, you could ask them to find a number on the ground and consider its composition. How can they demonstrate 24? With 2 claps for the 2 tens and 4 hops for the 4 ones? Can they create their own moves for hundreds?

There is much debate as to the order in which mathematics can be introduced. The most common approach seems to involve the introduction of the concept, knowledge or skill in the classroom, before consolidating it in the hall. That said, there are many reasons why it is more beneficial to flip this with mathematical understanding being discovered in the hall setting. One example springs to mind of a time spent with a Year 6 class in Durham; having completed the physical challenge of collecting a random selection of numbers, two boys – Jack and Lewis – immersed themselves in the thinking challenge. When asked, 'What do you notice?' Lewis replied, 'There's a pattern – it's a multiple of 8 plus 1, then the next multiple of 8 plus 2 and so on'. Nobody else – child or teacher – had ever made this observation.

When informed about the observation, the Year 6 teacher's response was: 'Lewis?! Really? He hates maths.'

As to other ways to deliver Move & Learn in a hall space, let's dance, dance, dance. In our interview with Jo Rhodes, founder of Challenge 59,[14] she states: 'Children's ability to recall, understand and articulate learning improves through dance. For example, by helping children understand complex concepts such as the laws of gravity. I have seen classes learn concepts from GCSE science and articulate the meaning of concepts such as the three laws of motion in an articulate manner. They understand the meanings of these laws and it is because they have explored this physically that they fully understand the concepts. Dance isn't just a way to explore scientific concepts. You can also explore issues – whether they be personal or environmental – through dance. Dance can change attitudes and behaviours (e.g. peer pressure or well-being) as well as boost confidence.' The impact of dance on confidence was also noted in a Department for Education blog post that referred to a student: 'a massive difference in his confidence, both in terms of his own movement and also interactions with his peers',[15] and in the systematic review 'Effects of dance interventions on aspects of the participants' self'.[16] Jo continues, 'In terms of developing an understanding of academic subjects, dance leads to improved vocabulary. Children can develop new words, putting them into context, using them in writing and communication.' This comment reflects dance's impact on writing, as seen in the case study carried out by the Royal Opera House's Create and Dance programme with Helen Moors and Hayley Ryan: 'children ... were writing in greater depth, using similes and alliteration, comparing characters, using predictions and incorporating speech marks'.[17] Similar findings can be seen in the reflections of teachers working with Siobhan Davies Dance: 'Dance is having a massive impact on their learning. Children are remembering stuff and articulating what they are learning a lot more than they used to.'[18] Elsewhere, Ms Knight from Horniman Primary School, while developing

---

14 See https://www.challenge59.com/.
15 Department for Education, Building confidence through dance: the teacher effect, *Teaching* [blog] (2 May 2019). Available at: https://teaching.blog.gov.uk/2019/05/02/building-confidence-through-dance-the-teacher-effect/.
16 T. M. Schwender, S. Spengler, C. Oedl and F. Mess, Effects of dance interventions on aspects of the participants' self: a systematic review, *Frontiers in Psychology* 9 (2018): 1130.
17 H. Moors and H. Ryan, Create and dance – unlocking literacy and the wider curriculum, *Impact* (12 September 2019). Available at: https://impact.chartered.college/article/create-and-dance-unlocking-literacy-wider-curriculum/.
18 Siobhan Davies Studios, Reflections on working with Siobhan Davies Dance [video] (9 May 2017). Available at: https://youtu.be/IEJlnezI4MA.

a cross-curricular project about rivers, notes that language acquisition is usually a slow journey. However, with dance, the acquisition is instant: 'I'm seeing my children pick up vocabulary from the instant they've picked up the movements … they've been able to explain what a "meander" is … They are able to use that in their writing.'[19] In our interview with Jo, she concludes: 'The processes of choreography translate to other curriculum areas. It helps children re-order, adapt, edit, refine and structure their writing. Dance also develops the ability to use inference using a variety of stimuli or ideas. Dance isn't just a way to negotiate space. It provides opportunities for children to actively listen, solve problems, make decisions and lead/support peers.'

Move & Learn outdoors

What the hall doesn't offer is the interaction with nature which, as we all know, provides both formal (learning) and informal (learning through play) Move & Learn opportunities in abundance. The main issue that needs to be planned for in advance with outdoor Move & Learn (or any outdoor learning) is how to deal with the weather. However, according to a well-known Scandinavian saying, 'There's no such thing as bad weather, only unsuitable clothing.'

Successful schools have used outdoor shelters (both purpose-built and those built by children as part of forest school) and also ensured suitable clothing and wellies are always available in school. We often get challenged around this aspect of developing Move & Learn as it obviously requires some investment, but installing decent welly racks for every class in the school is a lot cheaper than using PE and sport premium for new playground equipment or playground markings that are used for a few weeks, and then never again! Experience shows that the former provision will enable children to use their outdoor space all year round, whereas the latter will only be accessed by some children and provide limited challenge. Other simple ideas that ensure that Move & Learn works outdoors – even on a damp and windy day – are:

- Permanent Move & Learn posts for securing learning clues/resources for lessons.

- Orienteering approaches.

---

19 Challenge 59 (2020), Jo Rhodes Dance: Challenge 59 [video], (25 June). Available at: https://youtu.be/Z5CteBsxDqE.

● A Move & Learn shed (or, if funding allows, a box/tub per class) – to make resources more accessible for staff so they actually use them, rather than sitting at the back of the PE cupboard gathering dust!

Outdoor approaches allow for different experiences to those in the classroom. The outdoor space is particularly effective for:

● **Move & Learn Collection:** Children genuinely feel they are explorers/ adventurers.

● **Move & Learn Modelling:** for example, how the planets orbit the sun and the moon orbits the earth; in such cases children should experience all roles, as well as that of an observer or recorder of the process.

● **Move & Learn Connection and Creation:** for example, creating timelines along the length of the field or playground. Other examples include using the children as the concrete examples in maths models, such as sorting themselves out in Venn or Carroll diagrams. And remember, chalk is not just for the EYFS! Yes, chalk is often seen on the ground and the walls of outdoor EYFS settings, but does it have to be confined to the EYFS? Chalk is great for teams of children to run relays and write numbers in Venn and Carroll diagrams. Likewise, in science, older children can draw the lengths and shapes of shadows that change as time moves on.

Ultimately, outdoor learning can take many forms (forest school,[20] bouldering, den building, team games, journeying, orienteering) and they all involve movement. As Juliet Robertson highlights, the key is to keep it simple and focus on the quality of experiential learning.[21] Let's take orienteering as an example. According to Oxford University Sport, orienteering is defined as 'getting between a series of points marked on a map as quickly as you can, with only the aid of a compass and your own navigational skills'.[22] Great for developing fitness and compass skills, but in a primary school the potential for blending orienteering approaches with Move & Learn is enormous. With or without maps, children simply move from one station in the school grounds to another, solving challenges at each station. In terms of mathematics, this could simply involve a series of numbers at each station:

- **One number:** How many tens and ones? Can children double/halve the number?

- **Two numbers:** Can they add them together? What's the difference? What's the product?

- **Three numbers:** Which number is the odd one out? Why? (e.g. only number more than 20, only number with 2 digits, only number that is not a square number)

- **Four numbers:** Can they order them (e.g. smallest to largest)?

- **Five numbers:** What do they all have in common? (e.g. all multiples of 5, all square numbers, all prime numbers)

Alternatively, children could gather numbers from each station, then work on one of these challenges using all the numbers gathered.

In terms of English, this could simply involve a series of letters at each station:

- **One letter:** Can children write a word beginning/ending with that letter?

- **Two letters:** Can they think of a word beginning with one letter and ending in the other? (e.g. 'A' and 'G' lend themselves to 'amazing' and 'Ghana'.)

- **Three letters:** Can they arrange them to make a consonant-vowel-consonant (CVC) word?

. . . .

20 See https://www.forestschoolassociation.org/what-is-forest-school/.
21 See https://creativestarlearning.co.uk/.
22 See https://www.sport.ox.ac.uk/orienteering.

- **Four letters:** Can they create a four-letter word and list rhyming words or words with similar spelling patterns?

Alternatively, children could gather letters and/or words from each station, then work on a challenge related to all the letters or words gathered:

- Can they put the words into alphabetical order?

- Can they sort them according to word class or family?

- Can they use them in a piece of writing?

Schools should also consider how they can use Move & Learn across the curriculum in their local environment – making natural links with history (e.g. exploring landmarks, signs and houses in their community), geography (finding different routes to school, monitoring traffic) and science (exploring and investigating local habitats and living things). While there are health and safety issues to consider in relation to this, the Health and Safety Executive are actively encouraging schools to explore these opportunities with children as it is vital to their development that they learn how to manage their own risks in these outdoor environments.[23]

The benefits of Move & Learn outdoors are rightly being highlighted and championed by researchers[24] and practitioners (e.g. Nature Friendly Schools). These benefits include:

- Physiological – reducing stress.

- Psychological – improving mood and self-esteem.

- Cognitive – reducing mental fatigue and improving attention.

- Social – improving social cohesion and interaction in communities, as well as social responsibility in relation to care and protection of the environment.

However, let's finish this chapter by reminding ourselves that when we move to, between, with and from natural places and spaces, we are 'fuelling creativity and a sense of adventure, allowing children to experience the joy that nature can bring'![25]

....

23 Health and Safety Executive, *School Trips and Outdoor Learning Activities* (June 2011). Available at: https://www.hse.gov.uk/services/education/school-trips.pdf.
24 L. Keniger, K. Gaston, K. N. Irvine and R. A. Fuller, What are the benefits of interacting with nature?, *International Journal of Environmental Research and Public Health* 10(3) (2013): 913–935.
25 See https://www.naturefriendlyschools.co.uk/.

Resources that enhance learning environments

As teachers become more confident and experienced in delivering Move & Learn, they will want to start thinking about how the regular resources used in and around the classroom can be incorporated purposefully and effectively to make Move & Learn approaches an integral part of the children's school day. These can be broken down into:

- Everyday classroom resources.

- Outdoor resources.

- Bespoke resources and equipment.

Everyday resources for the classroom

If organised in advance, everyday classroom resources can facilitate movement within lessons without it needing to be planned into each lesson in detail – for example, if each child has access to a whiteboard and pen, a clipboard and a ruler, then many of the Move & Learn Collection and Move & Learn Connection approaches in the classroom can take place organically once children know they are part of their learning routine. This can be enhanced if the teacher creates a Move & Learn resource kit for their class, which could include:

- Hoops.

- Cones.

- Tubs or buckets.

- Number cards, tags or playing cards.

- Letter/word cards, tags or scrabble tiles.

They would then be able to deliver Move & Learn approaches more regularly, without having to constantly pre-prepare new resources. Teachers would then hopefully be more likely to adapt their existing planning to include the use of these everyday resources to facilitate more moving and less sitting while the children learn. The advantage of these resources is that they are a no-/low-cost solution as many will already be available in schools and, as they will be owned by each class, they will be more likely to be used regularly (and looked after properly too)!

Resources for the outdoors

Most resources for outdoor learning and movement are the wonderful natural resources that surround us (sticks, twigs, mud, sand). We appreciate that the availability of these will vary depending on your setting, but more and more schools are recognising the importance of regularly moving the learning to an outdoor area within school or travelling to a local woodland or park beyond the school gates. If you are keen to explore and develop this aspect of your practice further, we highly recommend you explore Creative Star Learning.[26] Here, you will find a range of resources and books that will set you and your children on the way to effective, purposeful and enjoyable outdoor learning experiences. We have also seen teachers use fixed orienteering stations (even with QR codes, if the technology allows) in different areas of the outdoor space. By investing the time and a small amount of funds into erecting permanent wooden posts for each station, teachers can plan a range of different activities from maths treasure hunts to retrieval of content from knowledge organisers. If QR codes are used, teachers can simply link the new problems or challenges to the relevant stations, rather than having to physically post the new clues each time.

---

26 See https://creativestarlearning.co.uk.

Bespoke resources

There are many bespoke resources for learning in and beyond the classroom, many of which have been created by educators and former teachers who have seen the benefits of Move & Learn approaches within their own settings and with their own children. Following successful trials, they have sought to widen the benefits to a greater audience than their own school. At one end of the spectrum you have the digital platform Nowpressplay, whose immersive audio experiences engage children with stories, sounds and music and can help reduce sedentary time as they can be used in a variety of places and spaces.[27] At the other end of the spectrum are the analogue tags of Tagtiv8, whose colourful letters, numbers and symbols are collected by children in a series of physical challenges (varying from light to vigorous, depending on the activity and the space used), before being used to solve various thinking challenges and/or blended challenges.[28] Standing – and moving – between the two platforms is Cross Curricular Orienteering, who map school grounds for children to then explore and learn about core subjects, science, geography, history and personal, social, health and economic education.[29]

Bespoke furniture will support teachers in transforming their classroom environment, so that sitting for sustained periods is no longer the norm. There are a wide range of resources available from balance balls, bicycle chairs and desks, standing desks and even climbing walls! These resources clearly have significant cost implications for schools and we would suggest that if you do choose to invest in any of these, you do so on a small-scale test-and-learn basis. As mentioned in the environments section, decluttering the learning environment and utilising existing resources should always be the first step, and any equipment purchased should be done with the purpose of facilitating movement – for example, if you consider using standing desks, research has shown that partial allocation can still be an effective solution; by only investing in a group of standing desks, it is not only more cost effective but can also be targeted at children that would benefit the most from standing for part of a learning session.[30] Included here are a number of possible suppliers that we have encountered, but we do not endorse any of these

27 See https://nowpressplay.co.uk/.
28 See https://tagtiv8.com/.
29 See https://www.crosscurricularorienteering.co.uk/.
30 A. P. Sherry, N. Pearson, N. D. Ridgers, W. Johnson, S. E. Barber, D. D. Bingham et al., Impacts of a standing desk intervention within an English primary school classroom: a pilot controlled trial, *International Journal of Environmental Research and Public Health* 17(19) (2020): 7048; Chen et al., Stand out.

products and would encourage you to only consider this option once you have really embedded all the other Move & Learn areas effectively:

- **Action Based Learning:** https://www.abllab.com/

- **Stand Up School:** https://www.juststand.org/stand-up/stand-up-school/

- **I Want a Standing Desk:** https://iwantastandingdesk.com/

- **Moving Minds**: https://www.moving-minds.com/

- **Stand Up Kids:** https://standupkids.org/

- **Sensory Processing Disorder Parent Support:** https://sensoryprocessingdisorderparentsupport.com/sensory-chairs-and-active-seating-tools.php

- **Yorkshire Purchasing Organisation:** https://www.ypo.co.uk/

- **Budget Standing Desks:** https://sit-stand.com/131-classroom

- **AJ Products:** https://www.ajproducts.co.uk/schools-education/active-learning-classroom/31980715.wf

Chapter 5	Environments and Resources – Moving along

Questions & Tasks

1. Is the classroom layout/learning environment flexible to the needs of the learners and what is being taught? How have you used different layouts to support your teaching and measured their impact?

2. What changes could you make to your classroom to facilitate more movement during learning? (Refer back to Chapter 3.)

3. What other spaces and places are available to you beyond the classroom, and what do you need to consider before using them? Particularly consider challenges and solutions to adverse weather conditions (which may impact on some schools for chunks of the academic year).

4. What classroom/other resources do you currently have available to support Move & Learn approaches? Do you have a budget available for one or two classes to trial resources that fit with your approach?

5. What sort of simple resources would help you deliver Move & Learn approaches in your classrooms?

6. Can you foresee any challenges of accessing/preparing/using resources to support movement in lessons, and what solutions can you think of to overcome these?

small steps
big difference

Based on what you have learned in this chapter, here are five simple ideas to try in your places and spaces:

1. Visit your classroom when the children are actually in it (e.g. during PPA time) so you can see for yourself how children learn in the environment. An empty classroom is always deceptive!

2. Consider how much of the furniture and resources in the classroom are actually used by the children for their learning/lessons. Declutter and free up space for movement or working in different ways.

3. Involve your children in co-designing and co-constructing the new layouts.

4. Plan a Places & Spaces challenge with the children; over the course of four weeks use one of the approaches from Chapter 3 to activate a lesson in each of the following environments each week:

    a. Classroom and/or corridor.

    b. Hall space (utilising free hall time – often in the morning!).

    c. Playground.

    d. Other outdoor space, e.g. field, forest-school area or your local park beyond school.

5. Set up low-/no-cost Move & Learn class packs/items to support the Move & Learn approaches you are planning for your class.

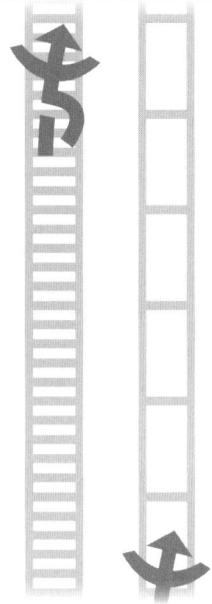

Chapter 6

A Whole-School Approach to Move & Learn

As this chapter draws this book to a close, we hope it's just the beginning of the Move & Learn journey for you and your school, whatever your role working in or supporting schools may be. There is exciting and innovative practice in relation to Move & Learn happening both nationally and internationally, but as highlighted in Chapter 2 (Culture and Ethos), for Move & Learn to make a real difference it needs to be embedded within school systems. This is why we were excited to be invited to be a part of the development of the CAS Framework.[1] This framework was developed in 2019 following a two-day conference at Leeds Beckett University, involving multi-stakeholder groups from the UK, as well as key countries internationally that have used whole-school approaches successfully. The stakeholders include researchers, public health specialists, active schools coordinators, head teachers, teachers specialising in physical activity, and active partner schools specialists. It was developed as a response to the fact that current interventions to improve physical activity in schools have been ineffective in sustaining improvements in physical activity – for example, despite years of investment in schools through PE and sport premium funding,[2] Sport England's *Active Lives Children and Young People Survey* (December 2019) showed that only 46.8% of children achieved recommended daily levels of physical activity.[3] This survey was updated in September 2020 during the COVID-19 pandemic, which highlighted that only 19% achieved the recommended daily levels of physical activity during the UK's first lockdown, and that the absence of school had a major impact on their ability

1   Daly-Smith et al., Using a multi-stakeholder experience-based design process.
2   Department for Digital, Culture, Media & Sport and Department for Education, *2010 to 2015 Government Policy: Sports Participation* (updated 8 May 2015). Available at: https://www.gov.uk/government/publications/2010-to-2015-government-policy-sports-participation/2010-to-2015-government-policy-sports-participation.
3   Sport England, *Active Lives Children and Young People Survey*.

to be active.[4] This not only shows the key role school has to play, but how much work still needs to be done to ensure children and young people are empowered and enabled to be physically active for their physical, social, emotional and cognitive well-being. In this regard, UK and global policies recommend whole-school approaches to improve children's physical activity behaviours. This has recently been reinforced by the International Society for Physical Activity and Health, recognising that a 'whole-of-school' programme is one of eight effective investments in improving physical activity.[5]

CAS Framework – overview

The CAS Framework identifies the components needed to create whole-school physical activity. It challenges schools to move away from just considering the interventions or opportunities in place for physical activity (e.g. playtimes, PE lessons, active travel). Instead, they are asked to consider the multiple layers that will ensure opportunities are targeted at the right children and have a sustainable impact – for example, an investment in new playground equipment may seem a positive strategy, but a school needs to consider the benefit-to-cost ratio of this; school leaders need to ask how many more children this will inspire to be active and how long it will last before it needs to be replaced. Conversely, an investment in welly racks or school waterproofs for every class, combined with a change in policy to allow access to the whole-school environment (e.g. school field), is likely to have a better return on investment and a longer-lasting impact on physical activity behaviours.

The following diagram (taken from the CAS Framework research paper) illustrates the CAS Framework; we will explore this in four key areas:

- **Policy:** In terms of national organisations' policy and recommendations around physical activity, and how schools interpret and use these in their own whole-school improvement planning, training and policy development.

4   Sport England, *Active Lives Children and Young People Survey Coronavirus (COVID-19) Report* (January 2021). Available at: https://sportengland-production-files.s3.eu-west-2.amazonaws.com/s3fs-public/2021-01/Active%20Lives%20Children%20Survey%20Academic%20Year%202019-20%20Coronavirus%20report.pdf?VersionId=2yHCzeG_iDUxK.qegt1GQdOmLiQcgThJ.
5   K. Milton, N. Cavill, A. Chalkley, C. Foster, S. Gomersall, M. Hagstromer et al., Eight investments that work for physical activity, *Journal of Physical Activity and Health* 18(6) (2021): 625–630.

- **Environments:** Considering how environments can be used and adapted to enable and improve physical activity.

- **Stakeholders:** Identifying how to improve stakeholders' capability, opportunity and motivation to promote and influence children and young peoples' physical activity behaviour.

- **Physical activity opportunities:** Considering the range of physical activity opportunities that are possible, and how to ensure the ones selected have the best impact for as many children as possible.

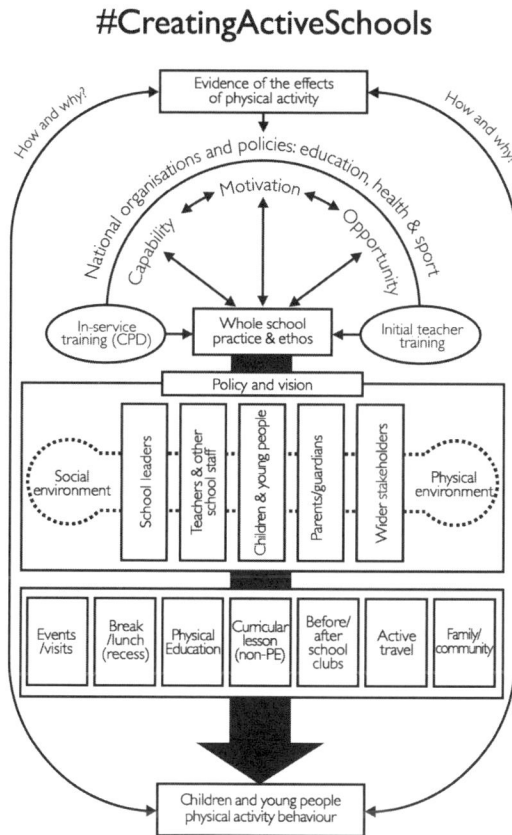

#CreatingActiveSchools

The CAS Framework[6]

6   Daly-Smith et al., Using a multi-stakeholder experience-based design process.

CAS Framework – policy

Before considering the school system, it is important to recognise the national organisations and policies in place regarding physical activity for children and young people, so that schools use evidence-based approaches to inform school improvement beyond just academic attainment. This is key at present, as while the research and national guidance state the importance of physical activity, many children are still sitting for prolonged periods in UK classrooms, creating a conflict between research and practice – which this aspect of the framework can help resolve. If we consider Move & Learn's role within this wider system, then the guidance from the Chief Medical Officers clearly places it as a key component of the solution for children at school, as movement in curriculum lessons will enable schools to 'vary the types and intensities' of physical activity across the week, as well as supporting them to minimise the amount of time spent being sedentary.[7] Furthermore, the first key performance indicator (KPI) for the Department for Education's *PE and Sport Premium for Primary Schools* guidance is the 'engagement of all pupils in regular physical activity'.[8] Move & Learn approaches can effectively address both these national recommendations, which is why we have developed this book and the supporting CPD programme that will accompany it.

Despite having this evidence available for a number of years, a key component to ensuring the success of physical activity interventions is ensuring school leaders and governors buy into the need to prioritise physical activity and well-being. In consultation with their stakeholders, they have the power to drive physical activity (and its related benefits) as a key school improvement priority that has the potential to impact on children's personal development, behaviour and attitudes, and quality of education. In relation to Move & Learn specifically, the opportunities here could include:

- Incorporating physical activity and Move & Learn approaches within the school improvement plan, as well as referencing both national policy and guidance – including key research that shows how physically active learning positively impacts both well-being and cognitive development. This is where school leaders can then ensure that other key priorities (e.g. teaching and learning development, curriculum development, pupil premium support,

---

7   Department of Health & Social Care et al., *UK Chief Medical Officers' Physical Activity Guidelines.*
8   Department for Education, *PE and Sport Premium for Primary Schools* (2014). Available at: https://www.gov.uk/guidance/pe-and-sport-premium-for-primary-schools.

subject-specific priorities) consider how physical activity in lessons could align and enhance their planning in these areas.

● Ensuring the school can strategically and efficiently monitor and evaluate the effective implementation and impact of its intentions to improve physical activity. As a quantitative measure, schools could use a set of class activity trackers to demonstrate active/sedentary times of particular curriculum lessons and then use this data to support teachers in activating the most sedentary aspects as appropriate. As a qualitative measure, they could obtain regular feedback easily from the children through both direct observation and discussion during a lesson, but also through verbal feedback from the children at the end of a lesson or as part of a monitoring focus group. Ultimately, if schools aren't fully aware of which children are active/inactive and why, then they will not be able to put in place interventions that improve outcomes.

● Developing policies and routines that enable Move & Learn to take place across the school day – for example, incorporating Move & Learn approaches into teaching and learning/curriculum policies, including the evidence for their inclusion, or adapting the school day to provide for more flexible breaks (Move & Learn Energisers) which will not only reduce prolonged sitting time, but make available learning time more productive.

● Recognising that initial teacher and in-service training in relation to physical activity is failing to equip teachers with the appropriate capability, opportunity and motivation to influence and inspire *all* children's physical activity behaviours. We have addressed this in Chapter 3, and we hope this book and accompanying training will provide schools with an ongoing programme that will provide sustainable whole-school impact with opportunities that improve outcomes for all children. A fantastic example from another country of an existing CPD programme that combines research and practice in relation to physically active learning, is the SEFAL Teacher Education programme in Norway.[9] This teacher training project was established in 2018 with an aim to provide students with:

> A more active, practical and varied day.

> More physical activity and less sitting.

9   Western Norway University of Applied Sciences, Center for Physically Active Learning (2019). Available at: https://www.hvl.no/en/about/sefal/.

> Physical activity as a method of learning.

The SEFAL programme combines both in-person and web-based training and support, along with a practice-based element so that teachers can plan, implement and evaluate Move & Learn approaches in relation to students' learning, as well as their own and others' teaching.

It is our hope that the UK follows Norway's lead and both national policy and initial (and ongoing) teacher training will more explicitly include movement-based lessons as a key strategy that can be implemented in practice to increase activity for children in the future. Work has already begun on this through the ACTivate Erasmus+ project, with researchers and practitioners from Norway, UK, Netherlands, Finland, Denmark and Portugal developing an evidence-based physically active learning teacher training programme due out in Spring 2022.[10]

Once physical activity (and, in our case, Move & Learn) has been established as a school priority based on the research and evidence available, it's then important to explore the environments that enable the policy to take place.

CAS Framework – environments

As we have shown in Chapter 5, environments change behaviours and the framework prompts schools to think about their own indoor (classrooms, corridors, halls) and outdoor (playgrounds, multi-use games areas, fields, forest schools, local area beyond school) space and how this enables and encourages children's physical activity. Environments are clearly impacted by funding available (a scarce resource for schools at present), but this is why it is even more important that funding maximises the return on investment. Rather than investing in expensive permanent playground markings or 'active mile' tracks, for example, schools pay their caretakers to chalk/spray temporary markings once per term, based on the children's feedback and how they are used. From a Move & Learn perspective, we have shown in Chapter 5 how to adapt the environments available to you, as well as recognising that the intensity of movement will ultimately vary based on this (e.g. indoors – light to moderate; outdoors – all ranges of intensity are generally possible). There is a growing appetite towards outdoor learning across the UK at present, which provides plenty of natural opportunities for Move & Learn; we suggest that the best investment schools can make here is natural development to

---

10 See https://twitter.com/activateeu; to find out more about this and subscribe for the free CPD, go to https://www.activateyourclass.eu/.

their outdoor space that facilitates its use all year round (e.g. wellies, welly storage, waterproofs for every child).

CAS Framework – stakeholders

Having considered how the physical environment enables physical activity, the framework then addresses the social environment that operates within a school – and how different stakeholders engage and support each other in enhancing physical activity opportunities for children and young people. It is important that schools consider the COM-B model (covered on page 22) for each stakeholder, as a way of identifying both successful strategies to pursue and barriers that need to be removed in relation to their capability, opportunity and motivation in this area. Let's take each stakeholder in turn and consider relevant examples:

	Example of capability to promote physical activity	Example of opportunity to promote physical activity	Example of motivation to promote physical activity
School leaders	Structures/roles in place to support increase in whole-school physical activity (e.g. specific link governor role, physical activity lead rather than, or in addition to, PE subject lead).	Clear physical activity strategy made clear to all stakeholders by SLT, with time for regular support, monitoring and evaluation of physical activity interventions across the school day.	Funding/budget (physical education, school sport and physical activity funding, pupil premium, fundraising from parent–teacher association) made available to support the implementation of the school's physical activity strategy.

	Example of capability to promote physical activity	Example of opportunity to promote physical activity	Example of motivation to promote physical activity
Teachers and other school staff	High-quality, relevant and individually targeted training for teaching and support staff linked to specific aspects of CAS Framework – in particular, delivery of high-quality physical activity in curriculum lessons and support of playtimes and clubs.	Dedicated staff meetings (delivered in an active way) and staff voice on successes and overcoming barriers together.	Individual performance management targets in relation to promoting physical activity in curriculum lessons, using research and evidence-based best practice beyond school to inspire and motivate staff.
Children and young people	Curriculum content (PE and wider curriculum) that specifically focuses on the benefits of movement, physical activity and active play beyond just health and fitness.	Children have regular opportunities to promote physical activity across the school day, e.g.: • Regular student voice.	Inspirational approaches, resources and environments made available in curriculum lessons and playtimes that inspire creativity and play through physical activity.

	Example of capability to promote physical activity	Example of opportunity to promote physical activity	Example of motivation to promote physical activity
		● Physical activity champions/ leaders. ● Students have facilities and equipment to be physically active in wet/ inclement weather.	
Parents/ guardians	Parent information events and training that support parents to promote physical activity with their children.	Parent voice is incorporated in the school's approach to developing and promoting physical activity.	School supports parents with the motivation to promote physical activity with their children, for example: ● Active homework or physical activity at-home activities. ● Home/school physical activity challenges.

	Example of capability to promote physical activity	Example of opportunity to promote physical activity	Example of motivation to promote physical activity
Wider stakeholders	Training from wider health organisations used to support all stakeholders.	Links with research and higher education institutions to explore innovative solutions to physical activity habits and behaviour (e.g. standing desk project).	Recognition with wider stakeholders and making school 'famous' – bringing pride, recognition and increased expectations to school community (e.g. regional and/or national accreditation).

From analysing this information, it is clear that improving stakeholders' capabilities, opportunities and motivations to promote physical activity is a long-term strategy, which takes us back to our philosophy of small steps and ensuring targeted intervention where it can make the most difference (and based on the capacity available to implement this). From a Move & Learn perspective, some small steps for each stakeholder that could support its effective implementation are as follows:

- **School leaders:** Showing a commitment to Move & Learn through school policies, and leading by example by incorporating Move & Learn approaches into their work with children (e.g. collective worship, assemblies).

- **Teachers and other school staff:** Implementing our Move & Learn approaches (see Chapter 3) in small steps, evaluating the impact and refining and building on the approaches used.

- **Children and young people:** Provide feedback on lessons that involve movement, so their teachers can continue to evolve their practice in this area.

- **Parents:** Involve parents in Move & Learn approaches by putting on an information evening on both CAS and Move & Learn, while celebrating high-quality Move & Learn approaches used across school (newsletters, assemblies, website, Twitter) and even setting Move & Learn homework for children so parents can be involved.

- **Wider stakeholders:** Our mission is to bring the wider stakeholders together so schools have high quality research, CPD and resources to deliver the best possible outcomes for children in relation to physical activity, well-being and attainment.

So, having considered the policy, environments and stakeholders with the framework, this will then strategically drive the physical activity opportunities a school provides.

CAS Framework – physical activity opportunities

The framework outlines seven physical activity opportunities as follows:

1 **Curriculum lessons (non-PE):** This includes all our Move & Learn approaches (activators and energisers).

2 **PE lessons**

3 **Playtimes**

4 **Events/trips:** Includes sports days, interschool and intraschool competitions.

5 **Active travel**

6 **Extracurricular clubs (before and after school)**

7 **Family and community:** This is how school can influence physical activity beyond school (e.g. links with local clubs, participation in local Park Runs at a weekend, etc.).

The order they appear on the framework (see page 101) is based on whether the school can control these interventions (from centre to the left) or whether they can only influence them (right of centre – active travel, clubs and family/community). In addition, the ones that have the scope to reach the most children and also have the greatest impact on duration of physical activity appear nearest to the centre. This is why our Move & Learn approaches are so key; they not only provide the greatest opportunity to get children active for longer, but also influence the area of the school day that teachers have the greatest control over. While children may have PE for two lessons per week, they will only achieve two hours (and this assumes they are active for the whole time, which is highly unlikely) of their recommended seven hours across the week. If you take into account the number of PE lessons missed due to inclement weather and hall space being taken (e.g. for school plays) then, while important, this is clearly not the way to get all children regularly active. Also, while some children will be active at playtimes, there are also some that will stand or sit for the majority of these times, making the use of our Move & Learn energisers and activators so crucial in providing engaging and inclusive physical activity opportunities for children and young people – which is needed now more than ever. If we refer back to the loss of PE lesson time, while we understand that this may happen, we need to support schools in replacing this with alternative physical activity (rather than sedentary) opportunities. Therefore, if a PE lesson has been lost then at least replace this with a physically active lesson (see Chapter 5 on some ideas that may support teachers in addressing this).

In summary, it is key when looking at the physical activity opportunities provided that they are inclusive and sustainable (e.g. low cost/no cost or one-off training costs), and ensure we are changing children's long-term attitudes and habits in relation to regular enjoyable physical activity.

Evaluating your practice and taking others with you

Our Move & Learn approaches are just one component of the multi-component interventions referred to in the CAS Framework, and as you move through your Move & Learn journey it is really important that you and your school see it as part of a wider whole-school physical activity picture that will reap short-, medium- and long-term benefits for the children in your care. Move & Learn sits at the centre of school-based interventions because:

- Research (highlighted in Chapter 2) has shown that it has the greatest impact on reducing sedentary time and can increase physical activity. This is because physical activity has a segmented pattern around the school day; therefore, the sedentary segments (e.g. lesson time) provide optimal opportunities to increase physical activity levels.

- Physical activity is a behaviour – you opt in or opt out. Compulsory time slots (e.g. lesson time) provide optimal opportunities to increase physical activity for all children, whereas discretionary time slots (travel, before/after school club, playtimes) will not necessarily impact on all students.

Given that Move & Learn approaches increase engagement, enjoyment and attainment, we refer you back to Chapter 1 where we question not why we use Move & Learn approaches, but why not? If you'd like to see how a pioneering school has got on with their own Move & Learn journey, we've included short case studies in Appendix 2 so you can find out about their successes and solutions to the challenges they faced. Move & Learn approaches will not and should not change schools overnight, but if we all take small steps to adapt our practice, policies and training to incorporate more purposeful movement into learning, then in the years to come we will hopefully see Move & Learn as an integral part of school life. We hope this book has moved the way you think about:

- How children learn and how movement can support and enhance this.

- Your classroom and supporting learning environments.

- How you adapt your lessons and resources to deliver the very best educational provision and experience you can.

Finally, we hope that you will continue to reflect on why, how, when and where you can find a way to help those you teach to Move & Learn. So, what is your next step?

As Nelson Mandela said, 'May your choices reflect your hopes and not your fears!'[11]

---

11 See https://borgenproject.org/nelson-mandelas-quotes-on-fear/ .

Chapter 6	Next Steps – Moving along

Questions
& Tasks

1. Refer back to the audit tool you completed as a baseline at the start of this book; complete again, showing how you have moved along in your approach to Move & Learn (including a reflection on your school's journey compared to the case study in Appendix 2). In doing this, revisit the following questions and tasks from Chapter 3:

   › Why do you create so many opportunities for children to sit down during the school day? What parts of the lesson do they actually need to be sitting down for?

   › How do you know a child is learning when they are sitting still and listening? Consider students' perceptions of this and how Move & Learn approaches might increase engagement and attention. Ask children to explain or draw what learning in the classroom looks, sounds and feels like for them. This could be done for individual classes, but also the whole school.

   › Discuss your own perceptions of barriers/challenges on implementing Move & Learn approaches and then identify practical solutions with a colleague.

   › Having completed the audit tool again, ensure this is incorporated into your school improvement and CPD plans going forward.

2. Consider the seven physical activity interventions referenced in the CAS Framework, and how your school uses these to make a difference to *all* children and their physical activity and well-being.

3. Then consider the five different stakeholders referenced in the CAS Framework, and how each of these contributes to positive attitudes and habits regarding physical activity and Move & Learn approaches.

small steps
big difference

- Complete the audit tool (see page 115), which is downloadable from our website (https://moveandlearn.co.uk/) using the code M&LAPP1.

- Make a pledge on the Move & Learn website: https://moveandlearn.co.uk/. We will send you a logo to add to your website, showing that you are committed to embedding active learning and play in your school.

- Watch the video from Creating Active Schools, https://www.creatingactiveschools.org/#video.

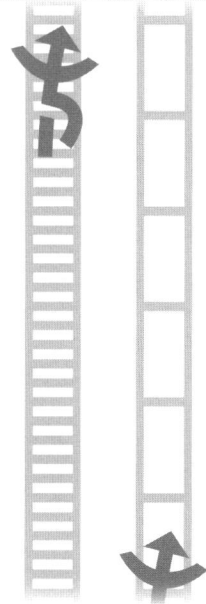

Move & Learn Audit and Planning Tool

How to use:

1 **Where are you now?** For each section (culture, approaches, resources, environments) start at 'Undeveloped potential' and highlight areas you've already achieved in one colour so that you can see where you are starting on your journey to mastery of Move & Learn approaches. Use quantitative (e.g. number of active lessons, accelerometer data) and qualitative (e.g. student feedback, staff feedback) data to support this.

2 **Where do you want to get to?** Use the evaluation from Q1 to consider with staff the next steps for your school in each of the four areas (including the tasks and questions at the end of each chapter), looking at the next possible small step you could take together. Highlight these areas in a different colour.

3 **How are you going to get there?** Agree key actions, considering how they change staff's capability, opportunity and motivation to deliver Move & Learn approaches.

A copy of this tool is available on our website (https://moveandlearn.co.uk/) for you to download. Please use the code M&LAPP1 to access.

Move & Learn audit tool

	Undeveloped potential	Small steps: CPD Possible strategies to move along the spectrum towards mastery include:	
Culture & Ethos	Staff possibly aware of research and policy on physical activity, but think it should only be provided through PE/playtimes. PE lead takes sole responsibility for this area of school life. Limited understanding of Move & Learn approaches and related benefits.	Staff training on the research and benefits of physical activity and Move & Learn approaches. Staff meeting to consider ways of enhancing physical activity: ● Active breaks to support children to refocus. ● Identify a lesson per week that could be 'activated'. Initial staff training on Move & Learn approaches – quick wins/simple strategies to try with your class.	Regular focus (at least once a month) at staff meetings to build on your Move & Learn journey. Staff share successes, challenges and solutions regarding: ● Approaches ● Resources ● Environments SLT support staff in developing Move & Learn by: ● Organising high-quality ongoing CPD. ● Providing coaching and mentoring on Move & Learn approaches.
Approaches	No or minimal physical activity outside PE and lunchtimes. Lessons are mostly sedentary.	Teachers use off-the-shelf resources to facilitate movement in one or more lessons per week. Teachers are aware of different levels of physical activity (low, moderate, vigorous).	Teachers work together to share best practice from trialling active lessons and then develop this through their own practice with the children.
Resources	No resources currently utilised by teachers to support movement in learning.	School identifies and trials a small number of low-cost/ no-cost resources to support Move & Learn approaches.	Resources that have been used most successfully now trialled and monitored strategically.
Environments	Learning takes place predominantly in the classroom.	Learning for one or more lessons takes place outside of the classroom (e.g. Tagtiv8 lesson in hall/outdoors). Staff try Move & Learn Spaces & Places challenge.	Teachers take learning in core subjects into the hall, playground and beyond – flexing to the needs of the learners. Teachers organise classroom environments to support learners' needs and facilitate organic movement.

		Full potential mastery
Research/teaching pedagogy used to explore where Move & Learn approaches fit into excellent teaching practice and how staff can develop their own bespoke approaches/resources relevant to their children, curriculum and environment. Whole-school review of physical activity across the school day from all stakeholders (students, staff, parents) – including feedback/impact and revised approaches.	Ensure each subject leader has Move & Learn approaches as a priority in their vision/strategy and are working with staff to identify best practice in specific curriculum areas. They ensure this is shared and embedded in all staff's practice.	All staff take responsibility for ensuring children are physically active throughout the school day and through engaging active learning experiences. There are regular opportunities for moderate physical activity to provide 60 minutes per day in school, and prolonged sedentary time is minimised across the school day/week.
Teachers begin to use their own bespoke strategies (using robust research and pedagogy) to incorporate purposeful movement into lessons. Movement even used to support home learning where appropriate.	Teachers share best practice developed, and support less-experienced staff in developing bespoke models that work for their children and environments.	Physical activity is incorporated purposefully into children's learning and play by all staff in a range of lessons across the curriculum.
Critical review and improvement of resources used to date – strategic purchasing and sharing of own staff resources (acquired or developed).	Staff start to adapt, develop and share their own Move & Learn resources.	A wide range of Move & Learn resources are carefully selected by teachers to enhance children's learning and physical activity.
Teachers start to design lessons that take different learning environments into account. Classroom environments are purposeful, adapted and flexible to learners.	Teachers plan use of learning environments to fit the purpose of learning and children's needs (not the other way round) using high-quality Move & Learn approaches and resources to support them.	Move & Learn takes place across a range of environments: ● Classroom. ● Hall. ● Corridors. ● Playground. ● Green space. ● Local environment beyond the school.

Move & Learn planning tool

When planning inputs, outputs and planned outcomes, consider and clearly reference:

- **Timing:** Short (this term), medium (this academic year) and long term (future years).
- **Behaviour change:**
  - > **Capability:** What skills/knowledge will be provided to change approaches/behaviour?

Inputs: What we invest (e.g. funding, staff release time, resources).	**Outputs:** What we do and who we reach (e.g. training/ coaching and mentoring of staff, changing approaches with children, adapting physical environments).	

> **Opportunity:** How will physical and social environments be adapted to change behaviour? What resources will be provided to support behaviour change?
> **Motivation:** How will values and responsibilities be aligned, beliefs challenged, goals set and emotions supported in changing behaviour, culture and ethos?

Planned outcomes/impact (e.g. capable staff with improved motivation, children able to move and learn calmly and purposefully).	**Evaluation:** Actual outcomes/impact.

Case Studies

School case study –
Birkby Infant and Nursery School

Paula Manser, assistant head teacher & Year 2 leader

Birkby Infant and Nursery School is a large school in Huddersfield that serves families from a wide range of cultural and economic backgrounds.[1] Physical activity and exercise have always been a huge consideration for our school; exercise for many of our children is done solely in school due to cultural commitments, social and economic backgrounds and the parental engagement of some of our families. Our head is passionate about the health and well-being of our children and was fully committed and supportive when we embarked on our Move & Learn journey last year. As a school, we recognised children's habits outside school are increasingly sedentary. How children spend their time in school is becoming increasingly more important. As the PE lead, I had a vision that physical activity should not just be part of our daily exercise, reserved for our PE lessons and 'Weekly 1k' (children run, jog or walk 1 km around our playground); it needed to become part of our daily teaching and learning too – hence the introduction of Move & Learn.

Views and perceptions

Bringing about change can be an incredibly difficult thing to do in school: children are generally willing to commit to whatever you offer them; staff are not always quite so keen to adapt and change to another way of thinking, another new approach, another new initiative. Throughout the year with various staff training, inset days, year-group observations and meetings, I was continually able to promote the Move & Learn message of the importance of physical activity within learning and the important role it plays in not only engaging children in their learning and the positive effects it has on their mental health but, equally, the

---

1   See http://www.birkbyinf.com/.

physical benefits it offers. The key to engaging staff was to show them how simple this approach really is. Many were initially concerned with losing control of the class, needing too many resources, not having enough space, lessons being too disruptive – only time and a different way of thinking enabled staff to see that this is not the reality. To develop a truly active school we knew we needed to: 1) create a positive, active mindset where children, parents and colleagues believe that activity is a central value of the school; and 2) create classrooms that aid PAL, not prevent it.

We started by decluttering our classroom spaces, creating room to be more active around the tables and chairs. We then developed active learning throughout the curriculum and lessons, trying to ensure that every lesson had a greater emphasis on the movement of the children while they learn. Staff were asked to consider what they did on a daily basis and reflect upon this when planning subsequent work. Staff are now in the process of considering ways to incorporate short active bursts of activity along with lessons that require moderate and vigorous activity. We also developed structured Active Play opportunities – considering whether *all* the children were active at break times or lunchtimes? All our Key Stage 1 children now take part in structured weekly active breaks led by our Year 2 play leaders.

Things to consider

Keep it simple, start off small and look for the quick and easy changes you can make:

- **What space is there for children to move around?** Could you change the layout of your classroom and learning areas so children have to move around it more?

- **Do the children always need to sit at tables?** Can they work on the floor, stand, write on the wall?

- **Does everyone need a chair?** Are there other alternatives the children could use to encourage greater movement?

- **Do your lessons create opportunities for the children to move?** Are the children expected to sit and listen while you deliver?

- **Where are the resources the children need?** Do you have the resources ready so the children never need to collect them themselves, or can you place them so the children can independently access what they need?

- **Assessment for learning – how do children show you where they are in their learning?** Can you create different body moves (e.g. red: curl up in a ball, amber: star shape, green: hands up and on tiptoes)? It really doesn't have to be thumbs up, down or in the middle – get creative!

- **Do children answer with their hands up? Or do you use questioning as the easiest way to incorporate activity?** Have children respond to a question or prompt by moving instead of just speaking if they know the answer. They could:

  > Stand on one leg.

  > Stretch their hands up as high as they can over their head.

  > Stand up and touch their toes.

  > Stand up.

  > Stand up and touch their knees.

  > Yoga moves (also great for multiple-choice answers).

Success

Active learning has been embraced by the children and staff in school. Staff feed back that lessons are more interactive and children are more active and engaged in their learning, and are increasingly willing to participate and share their ideas. Staff are enjoying the freedom active learning has enabled them to have in their delivery of lessons. The initial concerns regarding loss of control, disruption to learning and learning environments not being suitable have been overcome and, instead of seeing the difficulties, staff are now considering ways to incorporate ways to be active throughout each area of the curriculum. Active learning is great because it gets the children up and moving, which is crucial for their physical and mental well-being. Also, I can clearly see it benefits the children's learning as they actively learn to read, write, discuss or solve problems at various stages through-out a lesson. We have previously found that many children sit throughout lessons in a passive manner; by introducing active learning, children are now learning by doing.

Year 2 children tell us they love sitting on the beanbags and working on the exercise balls. As one child puts it, 'It helps me to concentrate while I am working, as sometimes I find it difficult to sit still'. Others independently take their work to the floor; another child notes, 'I enjoy writing on the floor, I find it easier to write my letters on the line when I lie down'. These methods may sound like a recipe for a nightmare, but they really do work. Our children respect the freedom to move that the active approach has given them. By using an active approach to learning, children are increasingly able to make their own choices and move between groups, activities and tables in a manner that makes them more responsible for their own actions, while allowing them the opportunity to learn in an environment that supports them in being increasingly active. Concentration levels have improved as children are more engaged in their learning due to this active approach. Some of the things they enjoy include writing on the walls, working on the carpet, spotting the 'crimes' in punctuation and 'speed bouncing' their spellings. Our journey is by no means over; we will continue to enhance our teaching through the active approach as the children in our society rely more and more on the provision that school provides.

Postscript: COVID-19

These have been challenging times for all schools, including ours. The difficulties of supporting families of key workers and vulnerable children, as well as providing robust online learning, are well documented. As we reopened more widely, discussions among staff recognised the need to build on the initial successes of our active learning pre-pandemic. We already knew the positive impact of breaking up sedentary time and making the learning more active and engaging. We quickly realised that by doubling our efforts in this area, we could also impact further on children's social skills, especially on communication. Play was an important part, as was using resources such as Teach Active and Tagtiv8.

Our vision to be a wholly active school is continually evolving. Being involved with the Move & Learn team has driven change and will continue to do so, ensuring that the benefits of physical activity and developing good habits early are a crucial part of our school vision.

Birkby Infant and Nursery School has since become a Yorkshire Sport Foundation CAS Centre of Excellence for PAL as of spring 2022.

School case study – Westerton Primary Academy

Jez Whawell, physical education and well-being curriculum group leader

Westerton Primary Academy is a large, three-form entry school in the Morley area of Leeds, with classes from nursery to Year 6. We serve a predominantly White British community with a wide range of economic backgrounds. PE and physical activity have always held an important position in our school. All teaching staff deliver PE lessons, including swimming, and they feel their knowledge in the subject is strong (as shown in our yearly staff subject-knowledge audit). This has been achieved through regular CPD for different areas of PE using the sport premium funding and, as we plan as a year-group team, experienced and confident staff are able to support their peers. Investing in our staff is an effective use of the funding as it allows us to have an impact on all students, which can be difficult in a school of our size. Funding was also allocated to developing a Play Leader scheme where our Year 5 and 6 students organised and led activities for students during playtimes. Participating in interschool sport has always been a big part of Westerton too. We regularly compete in a range of competitions against other schools in Morley, as well as Leeds-wide events. Although this has continued, it became increasingly apparent that only a fraction of our students were able to be included in these opportunities. Two years ago, we decided to develop our physical activity offer at Westerton so that all students would be involved, by increasing the levels of physical activity during non-PE curriculum time. I was able to secure occasional staff meetings in order to introduce new elements to the curriculum, such as active breaks between lessons and resources to aid the planning of physically active elements in lessons. Both were well received but did not become established; in order for it to become a reality, it needed to be part of the school development plan. In May 2021 we were selected by the Yorkshire Sport Foundation for our Year 2, Year 4 and Year 6 students to participate in Sport England's *Active Lives Children and Young People Survey*. Although we have always valued published data regarding levels of physical activity and health, gaining data specific to students at our school was extremely powerful. It highlighted the urgent need for increased levels of physical activity, and for it to become a part of our everyday curriculum – not just competitions, clubs and playtimes. It also showed that our students felt that they had low resilience and competency levels. As such, it became part of the school development plan for the 2021–2022 academic year. It also began the introduction of Move & Learn at Westerton.

In making such a big change at a large school, I knew that I could not lead by myself. I needed colleagues who would be influencers, as well as guidance on how to develop physically active learning from an outside organisation. Ian and Bryn from Move & Learn were able to offer support for both. During the 2020–2021 summer term, in preparation for the next academic year, the Move & Learn team worked with a member of staff from each phase in school who would then be the 'champion' to share good practice and support colleagues in their phase. We have worked hard to develop the Westerton curriculum over the past few years, so that it is knowledge driven. We want staff to become confident in including physically active elements in their lessons, to complement the subject knowledge rather than including something just because it was physically active. This will take time. The champions were guided through the direct and indirect Move & Learn approaches and explored how these could be included in a variety of lessons. As a group we then agreed that the Retrieval and Collection approaches would be the best strategies to promote with our staff first, as we felt they would be more receptive to them and be able to incorporate them across the whole curriculum. At the first staff meeting of the 2021–2022 year I was able to share the key messages from Sport England's *Active Lives Children and Young People Survey* and outline the expectations of how many physically active elements staff should be including within their timetable each week. This allowed buy-in from staff as to why we were making changes, as well as consistency through the school. The second staff meeting gave time for staff to review the strategies they have used and share good practice. They were also given time to share barriers they were experiencing and resource needs. In sharing good practice with each other, the staff were able to gain affirmation for the strategies they had tried or created, as well as increasing their own catalogue – especially with activities they could easily employ across different year groups, such as a Retrieval activity shared by Year 4 for practising spellings with an active movement for vowels and another for consonants. Equally, many activities shared by staff were longer activities. One that was well received was a Collection activity from a Year 6 class preparing students for writing their spy thrillers in the coming lessons: six hoops were placed at one end of the playground, each with a basic piece of vocabulary inside; teams of five then took turns to gather a word from the pile of synonyms in the middle of the playground and return to their team; they then discussed the meaning, as many of the words were new or unfamiliar to them, and decided which basic word to match it with and place it inside the hoop; the aim was for the whole class to sort the vocabulary accurately, rather than having a winning team.

The two main barriers the staff expressed were the timetable expectations and confidence in creating and delivering the activities. We have made good progress in overcoming these two barriers. Initially, the staff were concerned that physically active learning would add more to an already ambitious and full timetable. As with making any curriculum change in a school, there will also be concern from some staff as they are keen to incorporate the changes effectively but fear that it may initially go wrong. For both barriers, once they'd had a chance to plan in their teams and try out a few activities, as well as seeking support from the champions, they could see that it would be woven into their existing lessons without much more stress on time, and that beginning with activities that could be used in a variety of subjects allowed for repetition and becoming more comfortable with delivery. Collecting staff views for both of these was valuable to then discuss with Move & Learn during their next visit and gain possible solutions and guidance. During the same visit, staff were given the chance to discuss their views around physically active learning and how they were adapting to the changes made. This was beneficial, as staff gained reassurance and I was able to ascertain if, as a staff, we shared the same end goal. Ian attended our third staff meeting and led a session with our staff to review the strategies they had been using and align them with other elements of CPD they had received over the past year. This was to show staff that physically active learning is not a separate element of their practice but can be woven into and complement their existing practice, without adding to their workload. It has been well received as a staff. This has been clear from the discussions during staff meetings when staff have been able to share good practice and then suggest how this may work in other parts of the curriculum. Some staff have chosen it as an area to focus on for their professional growth for the current academic year. Also, from discussions with the champions, the staff in their phases have experimented with and developed the shared strategies from other staff and are relying less on their support.

Once physically active learning has become more established, we will need to explore the impact this has had on students' resilience and competency levels, as highlighted in the survey, and how to develop these aspects further through our active curriculum. We have found working with Move & Learn extremely valuable and enjoyable. Although our journey is nowhere near the end, I feel we have made huge strides in developing our physically active curriculum offer already, which would not have been as successful without the help and support we have received. We are excited to see what the future holds.

Lesson case study – Tagtiv8 English

This was a collaboration between Tagtiv8, Leeds United Foundation and children from nine primary schools in Bramley, Leeds.[2] Initially, the team took photos of various sculptures at the Yorkshire Sculpture Park and shared one of them, 'The

2   See https://www.connectingbucksschools.com/bryn-llewellyn-aspire/.

Man on the Moor' by sculptor Sean Henry, on Facebook and Twitter. Within days, they had collected words, thoughts and feelings inspired by the sculpture from teachers and friends (Move & Learn Collection and Connection). These words were collated and added to a slide deck, which was then shared with 20 Year 5 and 6 children on the Easter camp. They sorted words into sets: *known* and *unknown*. These words were colour-coded with a simple traffic light system. The children then looked at images of the sculpture on iPads and added words of their own. In teams, the children set about collecting letter tags via different physical challenges (Move & Learn Collection), before assembling the words on their Velcro belts in various parts of the playground (e.g. on benches, railings, gates, etc.). These words were then sorted according to the number of syllables, thus providing opportunities for children to connect further and create their own haikus. Some of the children also set about creating their own acrostic poems. Listening to the children, it soon became clear that they wanted to extend the creative process further, as they suggested performing their poetry to the parents. One child suggested choreographing a dance to illustrate the poems (Move & Learn Creation approach), while one of the coaches from the football foundation suggested performing their poems and dances in the Yorkshire Sculpture Park itself, thus bringing the learning back to its starting point.

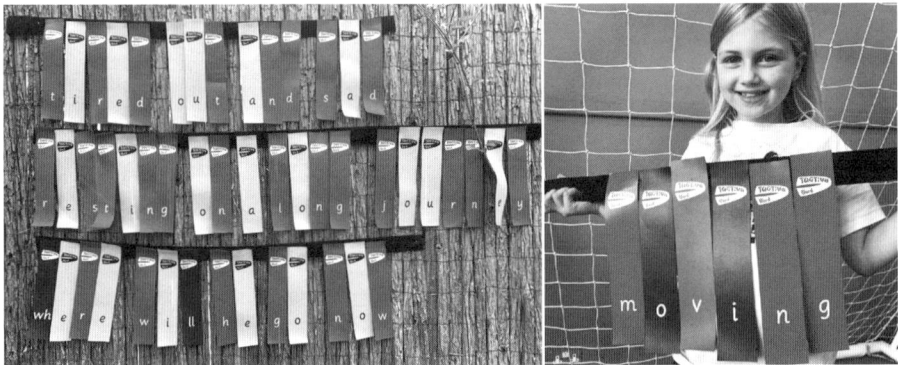

Lesson case study – Tagtiv8 maths

Following a successful one-off CPD and subsequent class sessions with Parklands Primary, the head teacher, Chris Dyson, decided to incorporate physically active learning into their curriculum offer via Tagtiv8 for one day a week, every other half term. This meant that they could introduce and embed active learning approaches gradually, across all year groups. At the start of the academic year, the Year 4 team – Tom Cunliffe, Niki Tighe and Jess Buckley – wanted to know what the children could remember about their three and four times tables from the previous year. The children were allocated to one of six teams. Each team scattered their collection of tags (0–144) on the ground so that the numbers were visible. As a warm-up, the children were challenged to hop over the yellow tags (odd) and jump over the red tags (even), saying a fact about each number. They were encouraged to think back to what they could remember from Year 3 and previous years. By doing so, the children were able to retrieve knowledge related to place value, number bonds and times tables, as well as one more/one less and multiplying by 10 (Move & Learn Retrieval).

The children returned to their team bases, where they were put into subteams. Each subteam was given a Velcro belt to hold. Their teachers asked certain teams to collect multiples of three, while other teams were asked to collect multiples of four. The children proceeded to wander across the playing area, talking about the challenge while collecting their allocated multiples and sticking them on their belts (Move & Learn Collection). Some children were challenged to look beyond multiples past 12 x 3 and 12 x 4. This involved counting on in threes or fours. Self-correcting was clearly evident when children began discarding rogue numbers. Watching the children, it was wonderful to hear one child say to their partner, 'We don't need to look out for the yellow odd numbers. They're odd and our multiples [in this case, four] are always red even numbers.' Back in their teams, the children were asked to connect and order all their multiples in ascending order. The pattern of odd/even numbers in the three times tables was modelled beautifully by one team in the mini plenary (Move & Learn Modelling). One team was frustrated by the fact that even though they had connected and amalgamated their multiples, they were still missing some. When asked where they could find the missing multiples, one child pointed towards the remaining tags on the ground and said, 'We can make them with those numbers'. Cue much discussion about which operations

they could use and whether or not they could use more than two numbers. These connected ideas led to the creation of solutions, which were then shared with the other teams (Move & Learn Connection and Creation). Further creativity was exhibited when the children devised a friendly competition, though not by simply counting the number of tags collected; instead, for the multiples of six, they decided that Tag 12 warranted four points (4 x 3), Tag 18 warranted six points (6 x 3) and so forth.

In terms of impact on the teaching team, Niki revealed, 'I love Tagtiv8 as it gets the children out of their seats, in a different environment and using new ways of learning. There's something about "moving" that awakens the brain and therefore brings joy and creativity to teaching and learning.' As to the wider impact, Chris Dyson has noted, 'We have children – and staff – who look forward to their Tagtiv8 sessions, now not just in mathematics, but English, science, geography and history. It's about a variety [of ways] of learning. The topic work we've been doing this year has included immersive learning and to be able to use the tags to spell the name of volcanoes, or the name of cities, again reinforces the learning. The science that we do in school brings out the rich vocabulary into outdoor learning. With research showing how important knowledge organisers are now, we can do low-risk tests outside using Tagtiv8 too. One of our Year 4 teachers even started trialling the letter tags in foreign languages. Watching the children collect the tags and create words in Spanish showed their versatility and creativity. As a school leader, I know that some teachers need more handholding than others. Many teachers and TAs are up and running with their own ideas. However, we need to consider how to strategically help those staff who need further scaffolding with active learning. We need to take – and make – time to understand their worries, their wobbles, their concerns. It's all about the long-term trajectory.'

References

Almondbury High School and Language (2013). Focus: Hattie's effect sizes; SOLO taxonomy, *The Pupil,* 2nd edn (September). Available at: http://www.asdn.org/wp-content/uploads/hattie-and-solo-The-Pupil.pdf.

Aubert, S., Barnes, J. D., Abdeta, C., Nader, A., Adeniyi, A. F., Aguilar-Farias, N. et al. (2018). Global Matrix 3.0 physical activity report card grades for children and youth: results and analysis from 49 countries, *Journal of Physical Activity and Health* 15(2): 251–273.

Barbosa, A., Whiting, S., Simmonds, P., Scotini Moreno, R., Mendes, R. and Breda, J. (2020). Physical activity and academic achievement: an umbrella review, *International Journal of Environmental Research and Public Health* 17(16): 5972.

Bartholomew, J. B., Jowers, E. M., Roberts, G., Fall, A. M., Errisuriz, V. L. and Vaughn, S. (2018). Active learning increases children's physical activity across demographic subgroups, *Translational Journal of the American College of Sports Medicine* 3(1): 1–9.

Barton, R. (2009). On your bike: what the world can learn about cycling from Copenhagen, *The Independent* (18 October). Available at: https://www.independent.co.uk/life-style/health-and-families/features/on-your-bike-what-the-world-can-learn-about-cycling-from-copenhagen-1803227.html.

Biermeier, M. A. (2015). Inspired by Reggio Emilia: emergent curriculum in relationship-driven learning environments, *NAEYC* (November). Available at: https://www.naeyc.org/resources/pubs/yc/nov2015/emergent-curriculum.

Biggs, J. B. and Collis, K. F. (1982). *Evaluating the Quality of Learning: The SOLO Taxonomy (Structure of the Observed Learning Outcome).* New York: Academic Press.

Caspersen, C. J., Powell, K. E. and Christenson, G. M. (1985). Physical activity, exercise, and physical fitness: definitions and distinctions for health-related research, *Public Health Reports* 100(2): 126–131.

Challenge 59 (2020). Jo Rhodes Dance: Challenge 59 [video] (25 June). Available at: https://youtu.be/Z5CteBsxDqE.

Chandler, P. and Sweller, J. (1991). Cognitive load theory and the format of instruction, *Cognition and Instruction* 8(4): 293–332.

Chandler, P. and Sweller, J. (1992). The split-attention effect as a factor in the design of instruction, *British Journal of Educational Psychology* 62: 233–246.

Chen, Y.-L., Tolfrey, K., Pearson, N., Bingham, D. D., Edwardson, C., Cale, L. et al. (2021). Stand out in class: investigating the potential impact of a sit–stand desk intervention on children's sitting and physical activity during class time and after school, *International Journal of Environmental Research and Public Health* 18(9): 4759.

Clear, J. (n.d.). This coach improved everything by 1 percent and here's what happened. Available at: https://jamesclear.com/marginal-gains.

Clemes, S. A., Barber, S. E., Bingham, D. D., Ridgers, N. D., Fletcher, E., Pearson, N. et al. (2016). Reducing children's classroom sitting time using sit-to-stand desks: findings from pilot studies in UK and Australian primary schools, *Journal of Public Health (Oxford, England)* 38(3): 526–533.

Coe, R. (2015). What makes great teaching?, *Centre for Evaluation & Monitoring* (31 October). Available at: https://www.ibo.org/globalassets/events/aem/conferences/2015/robert-coe.pdf.

Cooper, A., Goodman, A., Page, A. S., Sherar, L. B., Eslinger, D. W., van Sluijs, E. M. F. et al. (2015). Objectively measured physical activity and sedentary time in youth: the International children's accelerometry database (ICAD), *International Journal of Behavioral Nutrition and Physical Activity* 12: 113.

Daly-Smith, A. J. (2018). LBU research into physically active learning (ITV Calendar News) [video], *Tagtiv8* (20 July). Available at: https://youtu.be/Rd3hcPbYbss.

Daly-Smith, A. J., Hobbs, M., Morris, J. L., Defeyter, M. A., Resaland, G. K. and McKenna, J. (2021). Moderate-to-vigorous physical activity in primary school children: inactive lessons are dominated by maths and English, *International Journal of Environmental Research and Public Health* 18(3): 990.

Daly-Smith, A. J, Morris, J. L., Norris, E., Williams, T. L., Archbold, V., Kallio, J. et al. (2021). Behaviours that prompt primary school teachers to adopt and implement physically active learning: a meta synthesis of qualitative evidence, *International Journal of Behavioral Nutrition and Physical Activity* 18 (2021): 151.

Daly-Smith, A. J., Quarmby, T., Archbold, V. S. J., Corrigan, N., Wilson, D., Resaland, G. K. et al. (2020). Using a multi-stakeholder experience-based design process to co-develop the Creating Active Schools Framework, *International Journal of Behavioural Nutrition and Physical Activity* 17: 13.

Daly-Smith A. J., Quarmby T., Archbold V. S. J., Routen A. C., Morris J. L., Gammon C. et al., Implementing physically active learning: future directions for research, policy and practice, *Journal of Sport and Health Science* 9(1) (2020): 41–49.

Daly-Smith, A. J., Zwolinsky, S., McKenna, J., Tomporowski, P. D., Defeyter, M. A. and Manley, A. (2018). Systematic review of acute physically active learning and classroom movement breaks on children's physical activity, cognition, academic performance and classroom behaviour: understanding critical design features, *BMJ Open Sport & Exercise Medicine* 4(1): DOI.10.1136/bmjsem-2018-000341.

de Greeff, J. W., Bosker, R. J., Oosterlaan, J., Visscher, C. and Hartman, E. (2018). Effects of physical activity on executive functions, attention and academic performance in preadolescent children: a meta-analysis, *Journal of Science and Medicine in Sport* 21(5): 501–507.

Department for Digital, Culture, Media & Sport and Department for Education (2015). *2010 to 2015 Government Policy: Sports Participation* (updated 8 May). Available at: https://www.gov.uk/government/publications/2010-to-2015-government-policy-sports-participation/2010-to-2015-government-policy-sports-participation.

Department for Education (2019). Building confidence through dance: the teacher effect, *Teaching* [blog] (2 May). Available at: https://teaching.blog.gov.uk/2019/05/02/building-confidence-through-dance-the-teacher-effect/.

Department for Education (2014). *PE and Sport Premium for Primary Schools*. Available at: https://www.gov.uk/guidance/pe-and-sport-premium-for-primary-schools.

Department for Education, Department for Digital, Culture, Media & Sport and Department of Health & Social Care (2019). *School Sport and Activity Action Plan* (July). Available at:

https://assets.publishing.service.gov.uk/government/uploads/system/uploads/attachment_data/file/848082/School_sport_and_activity_action_plan.pdf.

Department for Education and Public Health England (2021). *Promoting Children and Young People's Mental Health and Wellbeing: A Whole School or College Approach* (September). Available at: (https://assets.publishing.service.gov.uk/government/uploads/system/uploads/attachment_data/file/1020249/Promoting_children_and_young_people_s_mental_health_and_wellbeing.pdf.

Department of Health & Social Care, Llwodraeth Cymru Welsh Government, Department of Health Northern Ireland and the Scottish Government (2019). *UK Chief Medical Officers' Physical Activity Guidelines* (7 September). Available at: https://assets.publishing.service.gov.uk/government/uploads/system/uploads/attachment_data/file/832868/uk-chief-medical-officers-physical-activity-guidelines.pdf.

Dorling, H. (2014). The importance of the school environment, *UKEDChat*. Available at: https://ukedchat.com/2019/04/30/school-environment/.

Follett, M. (2017). *Creating Excellence in Primary School Playtimes* [Kindle edn]. London: Jessica Kingsley Publishers.

Health and Safety Executive (2011). *School Trips and Outdoor Learning Activities* (June). Available at: https://www.hse.gov.uk/services/education/school-trips.pdf.

Hinckson, E., Salmon, J., Benden, M., Clemes, S. A., Sudholz, B., Barber, S. et al. (2016). Standing classrooms: research and lessons learned from around the world, *Sports Medicine* 46(2): 297.

Kagan, S. (n.d.). Kagan structures, simply put, *Kagan Online*. Available at: https://www.kaganonline.com/free_articles/dr_spencer_kagan/ASK38.php.

Karpicke, J. D. and Grimaldi, P. J. (2012). Retrieval-based learning: a perspective for enhancing meaningful learning, *Educational Psychology Review* 24: 401–418.

Keniger L., Gaston K., Irvine K. N. and Fuller R. A., What are the benefits of interacting with nature?, *International Journal of Environmental Research and Public Health* 10(3) (2013): 913–935.

Lewin, K. (1946). Behavior and development as a function of the total situation. In L. Carmichael (ed.), *Manual of child psychology*. New York: John Wiley & Sons Inc., pp. 791–844.

Llewellyn, B. and Daly-Smith, A. J. (2018). Physically active learning – improving performance [video] (16 July). Available at: https://www.youtube.com/watch?v=tARSCzHLF5g/.

Llewellyn, B. and Pukhraj, R. (2020). Why play is the answer to promote creativity and joy in children, *HundrED* (21 March). Available at: https://hundred.org/en/articles/why-play-is-the-answer-to-promote-creativity-joy-in-children#aee7cf5d.

Loughborough University (2019). Super Movers: schoolchildren performed better in tests after exercise initiative from the Premier League and BBC (7 March). Available at: https://www.lboro.ac.uk/news-events/news/2019/march/super-movers-brain-power-boost-bbc-premier-league/.

MacCallum, L., Howson, N. and Gopu, N. (2012). *Designed to Move: A Physical Activity Action Agenda*, Nike. Available at: https://www.sportsthinktank.com/uploads/designed-to-move-full-report-13.pdf.

Mazzoli, E., Salmon, J., Teo, W. P., Pesce, C., He, J., Ben-Soussan T. D. and Barnett, L. M. (2021). Breaking up classroom sitting time with cognitively engaging physical activity: behavioural and brain responses, *PLoS ONE* 16(7): e0253733.

Michie, S., Maartje, M. V. S. and West, R. (2011). The behaviour change wheel: a new method for characterising and designing behaviour change interventions, *Implementation Science* 6: 42.

Milton, K., Cavill, N., Chalkley, A., Foster, C., Gomersall, S., Hagstromer, M. et al. (2021). Eight investments that work for physical activity, *Journal of Physical Activity and Health*, 18(6): 625–630.

Moors, H. and Ryan, H. (2019). Create and dance – unlocking literacy and the wider curriculum, *Impact* (12 September). Available at: https://impact.chartered.college/article/create-and-dance-unlocking-literacy-wider-curriculum/.

Mullender-Wijnsma, M. J., Hartman, E., de Greeff, J. W., Doolaard, S., Bosker, R. J. and Visscher, C. (2016). Physically active math and language lessons improve academic achievement: a cluster randomized controlled trial, *Pediatrics* 137(3): 1–9.

National College for Teaching & Leadership (2014). *Beyond Levels: Alternative Assessment Approaches Developed by Teaching Schools – Research Report*. Originally adapted from Hook, P., Mills J. (2011). *SOLO Taxonomy: A Guide for Schools Book 1*. New Zealand: Essential Resources Educational Publishers. Available at: https://assets.publishing.service.gov.uk/government/uploads/system/uploads/attachment_data/file/349266/beyond-levels-alternative-assessment-approaches-developed-by-teaching-schools.pdf.

NHS (n.d.). Couch to 5K: week by week. Available at: https://www.nhs.uk/live-well/exercise/couch-to-5k-week-by-week/.

Norris, E., van Steen, T., Direito, A. and Stamatakis, E. (2020). Physically active lessons in schools and their impact on physical activity, educational, health and cognition outcomes: a systematic review and meta-analysis, *British Journal of Sports Medicine* 54: 826–838.

NSW Government (2017). *Cognitive Load Theory: Research that Teachers Really Need to Understand* (5 September). Available at: https://www.cese.nsw.gov.au/publications-filter/cognitive-load-theory-research-that-teachers-really-need-to-understand.

Ofsted (2019). *Education Inspection Framework* (May). Available at: https://www.gov.uk/government/publications/education-inspection-framework/education-inspection-framework.

Oxfordshire County Council, Oxfordshire Early Years Development & Childcare Partnership and SureStart (n.d.). *My Space: Creating Enabling Environments for Young Children*. Available at: https://www2.oxfordshire.gov.uk/cms/sites/default/files/folders/documents/childreneducationandfamilies/informationforchildcareproviders/Toolkit/My_Space_Creating_enabling_environments_for_young_children.pdf.

Piggin, J. (2020). What is physical activity? A holistic definition for teachers, researchers and policy makers, *Frontiers in Sports and Active Living* 2: 72.

Play Scotland (n.d.). Play Scotland Play Types Poster. Available at: https://www.playscotland.org/resources/play-types-poster/.

Ramstetter, C. L., Murray, R. and Garner, A. S. (2010). The crucial role of recess in schools, *Journal of School Health* 80(11): 517–526.

Rosenshine, B. (2012). Principles of instruction: research-based strategies that all teachers should know, *American Educator* 36(1): 12–19.

Ratey, J. J. and Hagerman, E. (2010). *Spark! How Exercise Will Improve the Performance of Your Brain.* London: Quercus Publishing.

Resaland, G. K., Moe, V. F., Bartholomew, J. B., Andersen, L. B., McKay, H. A., Anderssen, S. A. et al. (2018). Gender-specific effects of physical activity on children's academic performance: the Active Smarter Kids cluster randomized controlled trial, *Preventive Medicine* 106: 171–176.

Robinson, Ken and Robinson, Kate (2022). *Imagine If ... Creating a Future for Us All* [Kindle edn]. London: Penguin.

Schwender, T. M., Spengler, S., Oedl, C. and Mess, F. (2018). Effects of dance interventions on aspects of the participants' self: a systematic review, *Frontiers in Psychology* 9: 1130.

Scutt, C. (n.d.). 'Catch-up' and recovery approaches: selected reading, *Research Hub.* Available at: https://my.chartered.college/research-hub/catch-up-and-recovery-approaches-selected-reading/.

Sherrington, T. (2020). The art of modelling ... it's all in the handover, *Teacherhead* (November). Available at: https://teacherhead.com/2020/11/28/the-art-of-modelling-its-all-in-the-handover/.

Sherry, A. P., Pearson, N., Ridgers, N. D., Johnson, W., Barber, S. E., Bingham, D. D. et al. (2020). Impacts of a standing desk intervention within an English primary school classroom: a pilot controlled trial, *International Journal of Environmental Research and Public Health* 17(19): 7048.

Siobhan Davies Studios (2017). Reflections on working with Siobhan Davies Dance [video] (9 May). Available at: https://youtu.be/IEJlnezI4MA.

Sport England (2019). *Active Lives Children and Young People Survey, Academic Year 2018/19* (December). Available at: https://d1h1m5892gtkr7.cloudfront.net/s3fs-public/2020-01/active-lives-children-survey-academic-year-18-19.pdf?VersionId=cVMsdnpBoqROViY61iUjpQY6WcRyhtGs.

Sport England (2021). *Active Lives Children and Young People Survey Coronavirus (COVID-19) Report* (January). Available at: https://sportengland-production-files.s3.eu-west-2.amazonaws.com/s3fs-public/2021-01/Active%20Lives%20Children%20Survey%20Academic%20Year%2019-20%20Coronavirus%20report.pdf?VersionId=2yHCzeG_iDUxK.qegt1GQdOmLiQcgThJ.

Tagtiv8, Trying to influence the decision makers – NAHT & beyond (n.d.). Available at: https://tagtiv8.com/influence-the-decision-makers/.

Taylor, S. L., Curry, W. B., Knowles, Z. R., Noonan, R. J., McGrane, B. and Fairclough, S. J. (2017). Predictors of segmented school day physical activity and sedentary time in children from a northwest England low-income community, *International Journal of Environmental Research and Public Health* 14(5): 534.

Tremolada, M., Taverna, L. and Bonichini, S. (2019). Which factors influence attentional functions? Attention assessed by KiTAP in 105 6-to-10-year-old children, *Behavioral Sciences (Basel)* 9(1): 7.

Teaching Schools Council (2016). *Effective Primary Teaching Practice Report.* Available at: http://tactyc.org.uk/wp-content/uploads/2016/08/Effective-primary-teaching-practice-2016-report-web.pdf.

Tremblay, M. S., Aubert, S., Barnes, J. D., Saunders, T. J., Carson, V., Latimer-Cheung, A. E. et al. (2017). Sedentary Behavior Research Network (SBRN) – Terminology Consensus Project process and outcome, *International Journal of Behavioral Nutrition and Physical Activity* 14(1): 75.

Turner, C. (2018). Let children run around in class, headteachers told, *The Telegraph* (May 2018). Available at: https://www.telegraph.co.uk/news/2018/05/04/let-children-run-around-class-headteachers-told/.

Valkenborghs, S. R., Noetel, M., Hillman, C. H., Nilsson, M., Smith, J. J., Ortega, F. B. et al. (2019). The impact of physical activity on brain structure and function in youth: a systematic review, *Pediatrics* 144(4).

Vygotsky, L. S. (1978). *Mind in Society: The Development of Higher Psychological Processes.* Cambridge, MA: Harvard University Press.

Western Norway University of Applied Sciences (2019). Center for Physically Active Learning. Available at: https://www.hvl.no/en/about/sefal/.

Wiliam, D. (2016). Collaborative learning [video], *Education Scotland* (15 July). Available at: https://youtu.be/TqBNWEQmBRM.

World Health Organization (2018). *Global Action Plan on Physical Activity 2018–2030: More Active People for a Healthier World.* Available at: https://apps.who.int/iris/bitstream/handle/10665/272722/9789241514187-eng.pdf.

About the Authors

Bryn Llewellyn

Bryn worked in various UK schools for 25 years as a teacher, deputy head and acting head teacher. In 2012, he founded Tagtiv8. His pioneering approach to PAL (Move & Learn) not only provides an enjoyable alternative to classroom-based learning, but promotes physical activity – crucial when challenging the increasing problem of sedentary lifestyles. Bryn acts as advisor to the BBC and the Premier League on their education content.

Ian Holmes

Ian is a former head teacher who ensured physical activity and the related benefits sat at the heart of the school's culture and ethos. Ian led a school that developed a vision to be an inspirational place to learn and play, and the children and staff explored a wide range of solutions (e.g. active breaks, active learning, outdoor play and learning) to embed this approach within school life. He is passionate about supporting schools to not only Move & Learn, but to embrace a whole-systems approach to physical activity and well-being in order to improve physical activity habits, attitudes and behaviours moving forward. He is currently working for the University of Bradford, ensuring research and practice are brought together on the implementation of the CAS local, regional and national programmes, with his main role supporting the effective roll-out of the CAS Framework for over 40 schools in Bradford as part of JU:MP (Sport England's Local Delivery Pilot programme).

Richard Allman

Richard is a former specialist leader in education and SLT member. As a PE specialist, he delivered CPD to school leaders, teaching staff and initial teacher training students. Richard is passionate about empowering primary practitioners to integrate purposeful physical activity into classroom pedagogy.

All three are co-founders and co-directors of the Move & Learn Community Interest Company.

Move & Learn Community Interest Company

Our mission: to empower school communities to use movement-based approaches to learning.

We are:

- Pioneers of incorporating movement purposefully into learning, both indoors and outdoors, with links to current research projects in this field.

- Experts in the field: our vision, passion, experience and networks (in both research and practice) will effectively support you in improving health and education outcomes.

- Collaborative: co-design and partnership working is key to our ethos. Our belief in 'faster alone, further together' is reflected in the way we work – and play – with schools. Developing long-term relationships genuinely changes physical activity behaviours one step at a time.

We want school leaders, teachers, children and their families to:

- (Re)discover the joy of learning, both indoors and outdoors, seeking opportunities to make learning, play and movement irresistible.

- Realise and harness the long-lasting benefits of movement as part of learning – and play – on physical and emotional well-being, as well as educational outcomes.

Notable projects:

- Conferences (e.g. World Education Summit, Optimus, and AFPE conferences) and training, supporting Active Partnerships and initial teacher training providers.

- Provider of content for BBC remote learning.

- Collaborative pilots with a range of Yorkshire schools to establish our CPD model.

- CPD programme development for trainee teachers (currently working with Bradford Birth to 19 School Centred Initial Teacher Training).

- CPD programme for qualified teachers in 30 schools over two academic years (via Living Well Bradford).

- Collaborative Active Outdoor Learning project with 13 Bradford schools involved in JU:MP (Sport England's Bradford Local Delivery Pilot programme).

- Co-developed a physical activity toolkit for Madrassa schools in Bradford.

- Contribution to the development of the CAS Framework (July 2019 at Leeds Beckett University).

- Involvement in ACTivate – an Erasmus+ research project that will provide specialist free online PAL training for trainees and teachers.

- Outreach via Tagtiv8 to 400+ schools (and, more recently, to Living Well Schools' Reducing Inequalities in the City project in Bradford).